Secrets of the Caribbean Islands

Jamaica

Secrets of the Caribbean Islands

Jamaica

How to invest in Real Estate and Business

Andrea Hoff-Domin

Publisher: Florida Services and Information LLC, Fort Lauderdale, Florida

This book contains a detailed description of business and real estate topic. It is not meant to serve as legal or tax advice. For information about these areas, please consult the appropriate specialists—attorneys and accountants.

1.   Edition 2016—English

Photographs by Florida Services & Information LLC

Map by Microsoft map point

Cover photograph by Florida Services & Information LLC, Fort Lauderdale, Florida

ISBN: 0986252948

ISBN-13: 978-0-9862529-4-5

National Motto of Jamaica

Out of Many, One People.

About the Author

Born in lower Saxony, Germany, Andrea Hoff-Domin lost her father when she was a baby, and life with her new stepfather was never easy. Books about foreign countries and their cultures were her escape from everyday life and inspired her enthusiasm for the wide world. Her grandparents, especially her grandfather, had a big influence on her. He was an architect, and she accompanied him on his trips to construction sites and sat at his feet when he was drawing houses. At that time, she developed her passion for houses and properties, which is her main profession today.

She runs an international brokerage in Florida and is known as a Florida expert. To fulfill her lifelong dream, she started her career as a financial specialist in the biggest German bank and renovated condominiums. During that time, she began to write for several magazines and Internet portals. She lives by the motto "Do or do not; there is no try" (Yoda, *Star Wars*).

www.florida-dream-homes.net
www.andreahoffdomin.com
andrea@florida-informations.com

Contents

Why Jamaica?

That is a very good question, and I asked myself the same question before I went with my husband to Jamaica. We know Jamaica from James Bond films and the music of Bob Marley. The dreadlocks came also to mind along with the colorful traditional clothing with the head scarf.

We were very curious about the differences among the many islands in the Caribbean and the special features of each island. So we packed our suitcase and went to Jamaica to explore that island.

We live in Florida for years, just at the entrance to the Caribbean. We love Florida; however, it never hurts to expand the horizon, so we visited our next-door Caribbean neighbors.

Jamaica has already been on the tourism routes for a long time, and many cruise ships stop in one of the Jamaican ports. But not every passenger is interested in the geographic locations where the cruise stops. During a cruise, you enjoy all the adventures and entertainment on the cruise ship, and the attractions at your stops are often only a welcomed diversion from shipboard routine.

On every island are more things to discover and learn than you can imagine, and Jamaica is no exception. It has a long and diverse history, which brought cultural values from Europe, Africa, and Asia to the island. The Jamaican people embraced every culture and integrated it into their own as the country motto states: Out of Many, One People.

Therefore, pack your suitcase too and explore Jamaica for yourself. You will not be disappointed. This book will help you find your path to the treasures and opportunities of Jamaica.

This book focuses explicitly on Jamaica, and it gives you vital details about the real estate and business opportunities. The information is as accurate as possible, but for deeper evaluation of your individual situation, we recommend the advice of professional service providers such as local attorneys and accountants.

Accompany us on our discovery tour of this tropical island in the Caribbean Sea, with its mountains and waterfalls. The business opportunities are diverse, and the people are very friendly and welcoming.

In this book, you will see a detailed picture of Jamaica, along with its immigration, economy, government, and real estate. We are sure that you will love the island and come at least for a visit.

Maybe you'll like it so much that you decide to stay.

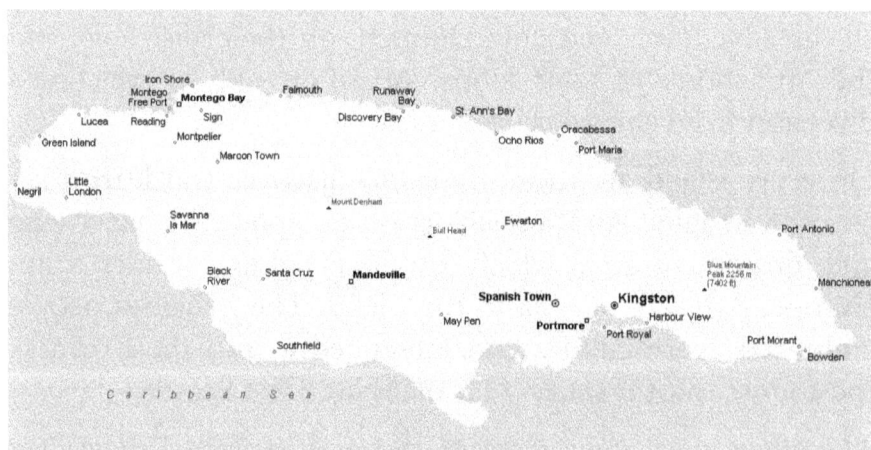

The Island of Jamaica

Secrets of the Island of Jamaica

Before we go into the real estate investment details of Jamaica, let us first explore the treasures of this island.

In the next chapters, we draw you a colorful picture, showing what you can expect when you make Jamaica your home, even when this island is only a temporary home for you and an investment for your money.

Geography

The island of Jamaica is located in the Caribbean Sea, about 90 miles (140 km) south of the island of Cuba; 560 miles (902 km) south east of Miami, Florida; and 180 miles (290 km) east of the Cayman Islands and 118 miles (190 km) west of Haiti.

Jamaica is on the opposite side of the Cayman Trough. This trench with a depth of twenty-five thousand feet is the deepest point in the Caribbean Sea. The trough is also the friction line between the North American and Caribbean plates. The location of the island of Jamaica is the northern edge of the Caribbean plate.

Underwater volcanos built the island of Jamaica millions of years ago, and during the submersion, a thick layer of limestone was laid on top of the volcanic rock. Volcanic rock and limestone layers are visible all over the island.

The island of Jamaica is 146 miles (235 km) long, and its width varies between 21 miles and 52 miles (34 km and 84 km). The surface of Jamaica is about 4,213 square miles (10,911 square km). This makes Jamaica the third largest island in the Caribbean behind Cuba and Hispaniola. The island is a part of the Greater Antilles and is an independent state, and it is still a member of the Caribbean Commonwealth.

The island has three different main regions: the Blue Mountains, the central valley and plateaus, and the coastal plains. This already gives a hint to the diversity of the island variation in the vegetation and the cultural lifestyle. Jamaica has many different facets to explore, and every little piece of the island culture is interesting and very lovable.

In the eastern part of the island, there are the Blue Mountains. The highest point in these mountains is the Blue Mountain Peak at 7,402 feet above sea level (2,256 m). On the distance of 9.9 miles (16 km), you come from the sea level to the peak, and that makes the mountain slope one of the steepest worldwide.

This mountain ridge is a national treasure and is an excellent place for hiking and bird watching. The view from these mountains is breathtaking. This part of the island is also called the higher land.

The low lands include the central valley with its two limestone plateaus and the coastal plains. The two plateaus are the Dry Harbor Mountains and the Manchester Plateau, which are divided by the central valley. These plateaus have limestone underground and are characterized by water erosion, sinkholes with disappearing rivers, caves, and grottos. The most famous grotto is the Green Grotto at the northern coast.

The third major area is named the coastal plains and has beaches and agricultural fields. The coastal plains are smaller on the north side of the island than on the south side.

The north side has mostly rocky coastlines with small and secret beach pockets, while the south side has beaches with the famous black sand.

The most famous beach of Jamaica—Doctor's Cave Beach—is on the west side in Montego Bay.

The island of Jamaica, like many other islands in the Caribbean, is a desirable vacation spot, and the tourists are coming either by air or cruise ship. The main airports for the island are in Montego Bay and Kingston. From these airports, the visitors are transported to their vacation locations throughout the island.

There are four cruise-ship ports in Jamaica: Montego Bay on the west side, Falmouth and Ocho Rios at the north side, and Port Antonio at the east side. From these ports, it is easy to explore the island and discover the natural treasures or taste the world-famous Jamaican rum.

Climate

The island of Jamaica belongs climatically to the tropics, and there are some specifics you should know.

The location within the tropics means that the island is closer to the equator, so daytime and nighttime are nearly equal the whole year. Based on this fact, there is no daylight saving change in Jamaica like in other countries across the world.

For instance, during the winter, Jamaican people live in the Eastern Standard Time (EST) zone, the same as Miami, and the time difference to London is five hours.

When the United States and European countries change to daylight saving time, the time in Jamaica stays the same. The only difference is that the time now matches US Central Standard Time. The difference to Miami is one hour, and to the United Kingdom is now six hours.

This information is important when you are doing business with others from across the world. When you come to Jamaica, the airlines have already factored this information into their airline ticket and flight information.

With the location in the tropics also comes the mild swings in temperature. During the year, the temperature sways between 77 and 86 °F, or 25 and 30 °C. In the higher areas in the mountains, the temperatures are cooler and swinging between 59 and 71 °F, or 15 and 22 °C.

The tropics also get the most rain in comparison to the other climate zones, and the rain is mostly concentrated in the summer months. The showers are heavy and usually short in time. The most rain falls statistically in May and October and comes with east winds from the open waters. Therefore, the east side of the island mountains gets more rain, while the leeward side of the mountains is often much drier. This rain pattern makes it possible that you have rain forest vegetation in some places in the mountains, and you should definitely make a trip to these places.

The high tourist season for Jamaica is during the winter months from mid-December until mid-April. In those months, the temperatures swing between 74 and 84 °F, and showers are less likely and less heavy.

During the summer months—May to October—the temperatures sway between 78 and 89 °F. These temperatures can vary in the different altitudes of the island.

There is also often a nice breeze coming from the sea during the day, which cools the temperature. This wind direction shifts during the evening hours, when the wind breeze puffs down the mountains to the sea. These temperature patterns make it more comfortable to live at a higher elevation.

The water at the beaches has a year-round water temperature between 81 and 85 °F, and it is always a pleasure to jump into the waves for a swim, snorkel, or dive adventure.

As already mentioned, Jamaica is located in the tropics and is within the hurricane zone. That means that between June 1 and November 30, the possibility of a hurricane exists. However, a direct hurricane hit is rare. The last big hurricane was Ivan in 2004.

Based on this information, you can expect a tropical paradise with much sun and gentle breezes, swaying palm trees, and white or black sandy beaches, that are well maintained and with beach amenities like showers.

Sunscreen for your skin protection is a good idea along with a light sweater for indoors. The humidity makes it necessary that your home be air-conditioned year-round.

There are no health risks on the island such as malaria or yellow fever. However, when immigration regulations for your home country require vaccinations, then your vaccinations should be up-to-date for your own protection and to avoid problems when entering Jamaica.

When you come from a region with yellow fever, you have to provide proof that your vaccination is current. There are no dangerous or life-threatening animals in Jamaica, although some plants and insect bites can provoke an allergic reaction that may need treatment. Antihistamine cream or gel is a good aid against the itching in such a case.

When you are allergic or sensitive to mosquito bites, use an insect repellent in the evening hours or after a heavy downpour of rain because, at those moments, the mosquitos come for dinner.

When you come for a visit, you should have travel health insurance, or you should check with your health insurance provider at home to see if and to what extent you are covered abroad. You are liable for your health expenses in Jamaica and must pay your medical costs out of pocket. There is no direct reimbursement or billing with your health care provider at home.

Ackee fruit

Flora of Jamaica

The term flora describes the specific plants and vegetation in a particular region—in this case, Jamaica. There are some particular plants that are important for this island and that influence the living. In the past the main vegetation was wood, and that gave Jamaica its second name—the country of wood and water.

In many parts of the islands, the native vegetation has disappeared due to the agricultural usage of the land. Jamaica was always the country that produces coffee and sugar and manufactured products like Jamaica rum, which is known worldwide.

However, there are still natural preserves and parks left throughout the island where you can see the natural beauty and abundance.

Along the coastline of Jamaica, there are different species of mangroves. They protect the shoreline of the island against erosion and offer protection for fish and other marine life.

At the south coast and at the west end of Jamaica, you will find swamp regions with crocodiles as well as desert-like areas with cacti.

To find today's natural preserves in Jamaica, you have to visit the Blue Mountains region with its native vegetation and the cockpit country at the northern part of the island with its mixture of plantations and native plants.

The national tree of Jamaica is the blue mahoe. In the past this tree was widely spread on the island, but due to its value as lumber and material for decorative carving art, the abundance has been decimated.

Another national plant is the lignum vitae. This plant grows in the plains and has blue flowers. These colorful flowers make this plant the national flower of Jamaica. When it is mature, it is a nice shady tree. Because every part of the tree can be used for medical purposes or in daily life, this tree is also known as the "wood of life."

In some regions of the island where the rain forest grows, you will also find many different kinds of ferns. In the Fern Gully near Ocho Rios, you will find both—rain forest and ferns.

Another very important plant in Jamaica is the ackee tree. This tree came from Africa with the slaves, and it is today the national fruit tree.

Throughout Jamaica, you will find a big variety of orchids. There are 220 different kinds of orchids to discover, and thirty-three of these are only found in Jamaica. The greatest variety of orchids is in the eastern part of the island.

Many of these Jamaican plants you will find in the Castleton Garden north of Kingston, but there are many other parks all over the island that offer similarly beautiful parks and gardens.

Fauna of Jamaica

With the island-specific vegetation come some very unique species that only live in Jamaica. These species have different habitats throughout the island.

Let's start with the most important species for Jamaica—the Doctor's Bird. This bird is the national bird and only lives in Jamaica. It is a hummingbird that has a black and green shimmering feather coat, and the mature male bird has two very long, remarkable tail feathers. During flight, these feathers make the bird look like a doctor with a flattering coat.

In the lowland forest, you will find the yellow snake. This snake is only to be found in Jamaica, and it is a harmless and not poisonous reptile that only eats mice and birds. Do not touch or kill this snake.

In the rivers, swamps, and the mangrove forest, you will find the Jamaican crocodiles. These crocodiles are protected by the law so that killing or hunting of them is illegal, so as an observer, you should keep a safe distance from these predators. The crocodile was always important for Jamaica. You can also see that in the coat of arms of Jamaica.

In Jamaica there are two sorts of native parrots: the black-billed and the yellow-billed. Both are living in the forest, and they are protected by the law. It is illegal to capture, hurt, or sell such a bird or to keep it as a pet.

Jamaica has, like the Cayman Islands, its own specific iguana—the Jamaican iguana. This lizard is the largest native land animal and is today critically endangered. Since 1948 it was believed to be extinct; however, in 1990 an adult individual lizard was found alive. Several more iguanas were found later in the Hillshire Hills. To increase the number of the animals, the Hope Zoo has a breeding program for these species. In the wild this lizard is protected by law and should only be watched and not touched.

The mature female iguana is fourteen inches; the male is seventeen inches long. The skin color is mostly green and blue with some darker olive-colored areas at the shoulders.

Another Jamaica-specific animal is a coney. It is a rodent and is living in the forests. They are one of the surviving native Jamaican mammals; however, you will rarely see them because they are night active. They are the size of a small rabbit.

This is only a small selection of the wildlife in Jamaica. There is much more to discover. You only have to look while you are hiking through the natural preserves.

Time Travel through Jamaica's History

Before Christopher Columbus discovered Jamaica as the first European in May 1494, the island was already inhabited by West Indies natives. The native tribe is called Tainos, also known as Arawak. It is believed that they came about AD 600 from South America and named the island Xaymaca. The meaning of Xaymaca is the land of wood and water, and that is the exact description for Jamaica even today. You will find lots of wooden areas and many waterfalls and rivers.

The Tainos were farmers who grew sweet potatoes, maize, fruits, and vegetables as well as cotton and tobacco. They lived in villages throughout the island along the rivers and coastline where they also could catch fish for their food. The native island population lived a simple life on their island.

On his second voyage to the West Indies, Christopher Columbus arrived on May 5, 1494, at St. Ann Bay on the northern coast. Based on information he had heard in Cuba, he hoped to find gold deposits and wanted to annex this island for Spain. The Arawak at St. Ann Bay fought his ships, and Columbus sailed eastward to Discovery Bay, where he successfully took possession of the island.

With Spanish sailors came European diseases to the island. The West Indies natives had no natural defenses against these diseases, and everybody died as it is believed. But newer studies show that there are still Taino descendants among the Jamaican population.

The Spaniards used Jamaica as a supply base for their conquest of the American continent. The ships from Spain brought food, horses, men, and arms to the island, and from there these goods were moved to the different outposts.

In 1509 the first Spanish settlement was founded near St. Ann Bay and named New Seville. The other town on the island was Spanish Town that still exists west of the today's capital, Kingston. At that time Spanish Town was also known as St. Jago de la Vega and was the government and trade center as well as the clerical center in Jamaica.

The Spaniards were not very interested in the well-being and support of their new island possession. There were disputes between the governmental power and the church, and that gave the pirates in the Caribbean a good reason to take advantage of these quarrels. They attacked the Spanish settlements and took what they could get.

Besides the pirates, the British also knew about the weak protection of the Spanish settlements and attacked on May 10, 1655. The Spaniards surrendered and fled to Cuba. However, before they left, they freed their slaves. These freed slaves became the Maroons, and they live today in villages all over the island.

After the successful attack on Jamaica, the British took possession of the island, and in 1662 the king of England granted the nonslave population in Jamaica the rights of

English citizens. In this proclamation it was also stated that these citizens could make their own local laws. The representative of the British crown was the appointed governor, and the legislation for the island was formulated by the house of assembly. The members of this assembly were members of the island's white elite. Their laws were mostly in favor of their own needs and were the source for many rebellions and uprisings on the island.

In 1670 in the Treaty of Madrid, Jamaica became formally a part of the British Empire.

During that time, many buccaneers and pirates were attacking the Spanish settlements in the Caribbean. They kept the Spaniards busy protecting their possessions.

The buccaneers' home at that time was Port Royal, which thrived under their leadership. The best-known buccaneer or pirate at that time was Henry Morgan who later became the lieutenant governor in Jamaica.

On June 7, 1692, an earthquake shook Port Royal and heavily damaged it. After the earthquake, many earthquake survivors left the town and moved to Kingston. Port Royal was only used as a naval base after the earthquake.

The British had a bigger interest in Jamaica than the Spaniards. The British settlers planted tobacco, indigo, and cocoa as well as sugar in plantations and shipped their crops and products to England and Europe. In 1673 the sugar plantations were booming.

To be successful and earn money, the plantation owner needed a labor force that was able to work in the tropical climate. The best solution for this challenge was African slaves, and so the British started their triangle trade.

In this trade, ships with goods sailed from England to West Africa, where the goods were used as payment for slaves. Then the slaves were shipped to Jamaica where they were sold to the plantation owners who paid for them with their own products like tobacco, sugar, and rum. These goods went back to England via ship.

Such a life was comfortable for the plantation owners, but not for their workers, the slaves. Many slaves ran away and stayed with the Maroons in the mountains, or they started rebellions and uprisings in Jamaica.

This constant turmoil with the slave population resulted in the Abolition Bill in 1808. With this bill the slave trade became unlawful and was ended. However, that only ended the trade, but it did not better the living conditions for the existing slaves who were still rebellious.

One of the most important rebellions for Jamaica was the Christmas Rebellion in 1831. This rebellion was led by the Baptist minister Samuel Sharpe, who is an honored national hero in today's Jamaica.

As a result of this rebellion, the Emancipation Act came into effect in 1834. In this act, all slaves below the age of six were immediately free, while the older slaves were released into apprenticeship. This apprenticeship ended completely in 1840, and the former slaves earned their freedom rights.

With the abolition of slavery, the booming sugar industry in Jamaica took a big hit and declined rapidly. The sugar production got too expensive, and planters in Cuba became the main producers for sugar. Low crop prices, droughts, and serious disease led to the economic downturn and resulted in social unrest in Jamaica. This led to the rebellion of 1865, which was suppressed with a strong British military force.

To solve the existing problems, the assembly turned to London and asked for a new governmental system. In 1866 the crown colony system was established in Jamaica. In this system, the assembly consists of the legislative council and the privy council, whose members were mostly British. Only a few Jamaican representatives with little power were permitted. The colonial office ruled the island through the appointed British governor.

Over time, this governmental structure was modified, and the white or nearly white Jamaican population slowly received more rights and responsibility to manage their island affairs.

Shortly after the establishment of the crown colony system, the capital of Jamaica was moved from Spanish Town to Kingston.

This new governmental start helped Jamaica to improve its overall economy and infrastructure. There were railroads, bridges, and streets constructed, which connected all parts of the island. The school and health system was established and improved the social environment.

With the decline of the sugar industry, a new industry arose: the banana plantations. Many of the sugar plantations went bankrupt, and the new owners moved into this new industry. In 1867 the banana export started, and in 1890 this fruit took over the leading position in the economy.

In the 1930s, Jamaica had to endure the same economic crisis like the rest of the world. The sugar prices went down, and there was an economic stagnation with huge unemployment, low wages, high prices, and poor living conditions. Unrest, riots, and violence were common at that time, and Jamaica requested an economic development program from England in its crown colony rulings.

During that time, the political parties of Jamaica were founded by William Bustamante and Norman Manley. Their goal was the self-determination of the island.

In 1938 the Moyne Commission was established and put in charge of examining the economic challenges. Their findings resulted in better wages and a new constitution. This new constitution was issued on November 20, 1944. It modified the crown colony ruling system. The island got limited self-government rights as well as ministerial responsibility and rule of law.

The first election for the thirty-two members of the house of representatives under the new constitution took place in 1944; however, the ultimate power still remained with the British governor and other high officials.

Between 1944 and 1962, Jamaica explored their limited self-government and their option to become an independent nation. Based on their cultural background, the people of Jamaica preferred the British culture; however, they disliked the domination and the dictatorial advice of the British colonial office. During these years, the Jamaican parties fought for more independence and government rights, which were slowly granted by the British government.

Besides Jamaica, other British crown colonies also wanted to get more self-government and independence rights, but Great Britain only intended to grant such rights to the crown colonies as a whole and not to an individual island. For this purpose, the West Indies Federation was founded in 1958, and Jamaica was one of the members at that time.

In a referendum in 1961, the Jamaican people decided to leave the federation, which was dissolved in 1962. On August 6, 1962, Jamaica became an independent state with its own parliamentary system; however, it remains in the Commonwealth of Nations. Because Jamaica is a member of the Commonwealth, the monarch of Great Britain is also the head of the state of Jamaica, and the monarch's representative is the appointed general governor.

Until the 1950s, Jamaica produced mostly agricultural goods like coffee, sugar, and bananas. Up to the 1970s, this agricultural dependency decreased, and the industrial products like bauxite mining increased.

To reduce the dependency from agricultural production, Jamaica was looking for other income-producing sectors. One of these industry sectors was music with its stars like Bob Marley, Peter Tosh, and others.

Another one was the film industry, which started in 1972. However, a film does not always have to be produced completely in Jamaica to become famous. For example, parts of James Bond films were produced on the island, because in this tropical location, you can find nearly every scenery needed: beaches, caves, mountains, wide beach roads with the view to the open water, or terrific views from the mountain peaks to the open waters as well as marinas with private boats.

The tourism industry is another very important sector for the country. Today about 60 percent of the GDP in Jamaica comes from tourism; however, most of this money is income for multinational resort companies and does not stay in the country.

The visitors come either by air or cruise ship and start their island trips from the different ports. Connected to the tourism industry is the second-home market in the tourist centers. This market is just starting and growing, and it offers many opportunities for buyers and investors.

In the 1970s and 1980s, the Jamaican government reformed the education system to provide better job opportunities in the government sector for a broader group of the population.

With this reform came the land reform and the introduction of minimum wage regulation, equal pay for women, and social components like maternity leave. There were programs to stimulate the private business sectors as well as the housing sector with its housing trust. The infrastructure and the health system were reformed and improved too.

Depending on the political party that governed Jamaica, there was either more private or more governmental involvement in these reforms. With the change of the governing party, the external connection also shifted, and the country was either more strongly connected to the United States during the Reagan era or more to countries like Cuba and other socialistic nations.

Jamaica still struggles with its financial obligations, but it does not give up. The sugar export to Europe, which is about 25 percent, is influenced by changing EU regulations, and so Jamaica has to replace this industry with a different industry because it cannot compete within those regulations.

One option is the production of marijuana. Since February 2015, it is legal to grow up to five plants for personal use and have up to two ounces in your possession. In connection with this law, the government also put regulations in place for the cultivation and distribution of cannabis for medical and religious reasons. Jamaica hopes to generate income with this new product.

Since 1969 Jamaica has had its own currency: the Jamaica dollar or J$. You are encouraged to exchange your US dollars into Jamaica dollars to pay for your personal expenses in Jamaica. However, in many shops, malls, museums, and resorts, you can also pay with US dollars.

The conversion from US dollars to Jamaica dollars is floating on a daily basis. For example, on November 4, 2015, the conversion was US$1.00 equals J$119.73. You can get your cash directly from every ATM that accepts US credit cards as well as debit cards. However, you should always check with your bank in your home country to see if your card will be accepted and if there are any bank fees or charges involved with such a transaction.

Since the independence in August 1962, Jamaica has had its own flag without any symbols of the United Kingdom, even when the nation is still a member of the Commonwealth of Nations.

The flag consists of a gold diagonal cross and four triangles in green and black. The green triangles are at the top and the bottom of the flag, while the black ones are on the right and left side of the flag.

The meaning of this design is as follows: the golden cross symbols the sunshine and the natural resources; the green triangles stand for the richness of the land and the hope, while the black triangles are the symbol for the strength and the creativity of the people.

Jamaican Flag

Culture Respect to the Jamaican People

When you are in Jamaica, please keep in mind that you are a guest in a foreign country and that the Jamaican population has a different cultural background and experience than you do. The best way to make friends and feel comfortable is to observe and adapt your personal behavior during your stay on the island.

Like every other population, the Jamaicans are proud of their country, their accomplishments, and their flag; therefore, show respect to the flag. Do not use the flag in an inappropriate or disrespectful manner, because it is a symbol of the country and the people.

The country motto and the coat of arms also show the pride and the diversity of the Jamaican people.

The country motto is Out of Many, One People. This motto describes the diversity of the people of Jamaica. Their original population were West Indies natives from South America. With the Spaniards, the first Europeans were mixed in and then followed people from England, West Africa, India, and China. Over the centuries, this diverse population formed the Jamaican people.

The coat of arms consists of two Tainos—a man and a woman—on each side of the coat of arms shield. On the shield, you see a red cross on a white ground with five pineapples—which are also cultivated in Jamaica. On top of the shield there is the royal helmet as a symbol for the British connection. The royal helmet is crowned with a Jamaican crocodile.

The people of Jamaica are always polite and respectful to you. When you meet them on the street, they will greet you with "Good morning" or "Good afternoon." That is the best way to start a conversation.

If you know the first name of your conversation partner, you can include a "Miss" or "Mister" before the name. That is a respectful way of addressing a person.

For the Jamaicans, status is important, and they expect the same from their counterparts. A formal handshake with eye contact and a smile is the right way to start a meeting.

However, the Jamaicans do speak freely and openly. Therefore, do not be surprised when you hear words that might not be appropriate or politically correct in your country—it is just the Jamaican way to talk.

The business language is English. However, based on the population mixture, you will also hear embedded words from Spanish and African dialects. This language is called a patois or Jamaican creole. This specific language is often used in Jamaican music.

As mentioned earlier, Jamaica does not have daylight saving time. That means that when you are, for example, from New York and are on the islands during the winter months, then you do not need to adjust your watch. When you are in Jamaica during the summer months, then you have to turn your watch back one hour, because in New York there is daylight saving time but not in Jamaica.

The usual business hours for shops and other service providers are 8:30 a.m. to 5:00 p.m. on weekdays. Some businesses operate on Saturdays, too, but have different opening hours. Postal and government offices and bank branches are usually closed on Saturdays. On Sundays all businesses are closed. You cannot shop on Sundays, as you may be used to in your home country.

Restaurants and bar opening hours vary from location to location. Usually they open at the early evening hours for dinner or happy hour, and you have check when they close.

The gratuity for the service in restaurants and bars is often included and added to your check. You will find a note at the bottom of your check that states the amount of tip. A common percentage is 10 to 15 percent of the total. If the tip is not included, the common amount is between 10 and 20 percent of the check balance.

The doorman gets one dollar per bag, and the housekeeper gets one dollar per person for her room service per night.

When you stop a taxi on the street, expect to pay a tip of 10 to 15 percent on top of the meter amount. During the nighttime hours, the tip is up to 25 percent, so check with the driver before you board the taxi.

Jamaica has sales tax of 16 ½ percent added to products and services in hotels and restaurants. For hotel rooms, a national accommodation fee is due. Additionally there may be some municipality fees or charges in hotels that vary from location to location. However, all charges and fees are documented on your invoice.

When you go shopping, please keep in mind, haggling is only common in some local shops. You should only start haggling when you are really interested in the item to avoid bad experiences. Please also keep in mind, when you are shopping in crafts markets for local products, these products are often handmade in the colorful Jamaican style.

When you want to shop without haggling, the duty-free shops or the big retail malls are the best options for you. Their prices are fixed unless they have a special sale promotion.

In Jamaica you can choose among all kinds of foods from all parts of the world; however, the original Jamaican dishes are also very tasty. They are influenced by African and Indian food preparation and ingredients. Besides the usual restaurants, you can also try the jerk huts that are along beaches or roads. Their cooking facility is normally a steel drum grill. You buy their traditional Jamaican dishes and take them with you.

The typical local food is curry goat or ackee and saltfish. The goat dishes will be understandable, when you drive through the countryside. Often you will see goats at the roadside peacefully eating the grass. You should be careful driving, because sometimes the goats unexpectedly cross the roads.

Besides many other music styles in Jamaica, reggae is the most famous. Music in Jamaica is not only for entertainment, but it is also used to express yourself. This trend had evolved in the 1960s from the traditional music styles in Jamaica, and the best-known performers for this kind of music are Bob Marley and Peter Tosh. To get more information about this music style and the history, you can visit the Bob Marley Museum in Kingston.

The country of Jamaica can also be the business location you are looking for. However, to be successful in the business environment in Jamaica, you have to understand that the easy-going dress code does not apply in this part of life.

For business appointments, a business dress and jacketed suits are the way to go. The colors should be kept in the conservative range and style. In the evening, the dress code in hotels and restaurants is elegant and stylish, but not too revealing. In Kingston the fashion style is more upscale than in Montego Bay, Negril, or Ocho Rios. In the latter cities, you can go more with the Jamaican-style colorful outfits.

It is definitely not appropriate to walk in swimwear along the streets, as you might do that in some other countries. You should always cover your swimwear with long shorts and a T-shirt or a beach dress. To such an outfit—especially when you choose to dress in the colorful Jamaican style, a hat and sunglasses are excellent accessories.

At the public beaches, topless sunbathing or nudity is strictly forbidden, and it is good guest manners to respect these rules and cover your personal treasures.

The Jamaicans are strongly family oriented, and to the close family belong aunts and uncles as well as nephews and nieces. The family meetings are important and offer the social support, and the financial support, if needed.

This tight relationship can also include close friends, when there is a trustworthy connection between the partners. In such a connection, it is also common to help each other to raise money for a big purchase like a house or a business, because the usual Jamaican has a trust issue with authority.

This shows that the Caribbean charm of the past still exists, and Jamaica has a lot of its historical charm preserved. Come and make your own experience. You will not regret it, because Jamaica has much to offer.

Country Products of Jamaica

Since the first settlers came to the island, the main products have come from the land and the plants. Jamaica is the land of wood and water as already mentioned, and therefore the main products are based on these resources.

In a former time, Jamaica was an agricultural region, and all export products were grown locally and exported to England.

The traditional products at that time were sugar, indigo, and rum. Later, cocoa, pineapple, and bananas were grown on the island.

These products are cultivated on big plantations that were owned by British planters in the past. Some of these plantations still exist and produce even now. However, they have expanded their services to include tourism.

In some of these plantations, you can stay as a paying guest and experience the plantation lifestyle. The plantation staff will pick you up and drive you to the plantation facility, because the rooms or apartments are often located within the field and in the mountains.

Other handmade products are Jamaican traditional clothing. These dresses are made from high-quality, woven, colorful calico plaid and often in combinations of white, green, red, and yellow cotton material. The accessories are the head scarf matching to the dress. The men's clothing is similarly colorful; however, they have a hat instead of a head scarf. The color range is based on the Rastafarian tradition.

Besides the colorful clothing, you can buy handmade baskets, purses, hats, and much more in the above-mentioned colors.

As mentioned in the chapter about the Jamaican flora, the national tree on the island is lignum vitae wood, and the wood of this tree is an excellent material for decorative wood carvings that are sold in the craft markets.

Many local painters and photographers sell their products with scenes of the Jamaican nature and life in these craft markets too. You will certainly find something nice for your home.

Maybe you like to enjoy a cup of coffee, and in Jamaica you will find a very good one: the Blue Mountain Coffee. This coffee has been cultivated since 1885 and has different blends to choose from.

Another famous Jamaican product is the Tia Maria coffee liqueur, which is based on the Blue Mountain Coffee.

Not to forget the different flavors of the Appleton rum products. When you make a rum tour to the Appleton Estate in the Nassau Valley, you can taste all of them and find out which one you like most.

You can buy all these products at the local arts and crafts markets and local stores at different locations throughout the island.

Transportation and Driving in Jamaica

When you are in Jamaica, you have different options to go from point A to point B. The easiest way is to drive yourself. You need to keep in mind, Jamaica was in a former time a crown colony and has kept the driving habits from that time. The traffic rules are based on the British driving rules, but there are some deviations to consider.

You have to drive on the left side of the road, and that can be tough at first, especially when you are from a country where you drive on the right side of the road.

You don't always have a middle lane in the roads, for the right turns into a road or into a property entrance. Always be careful when passing in such a situation, because sometimes the driver pulls back because he made a mistake or lost his direction.

When you come to a four-way stop, the cars drive as they arrive. That means the car that arrives first, drives ahead first. Please be cautious when you look at the car's turn signal; not every driver is perfect in showing his or her directional signal or does not use the turn signal at all.

You as the driver also have to adjust to your car's instruments. When your car has the steering wheel on the right side, the turning signal and the window wipers are reversed, and that can be very confusing at the beginning.

In Jamaica you have only a few roundabouts to direct traffic. Please keep in mind, when you enter into a roundabout, drive clockwise and give way to the traffic that is already in the roundabout.

These are simple rules, and everybody knows them, because they apply not only in Jamaica but in many other countries too. The biggest issue is that you must always keep in mind to drive on the left side of the road. The driving on the left side can be a stress factor especially when intoxicated. In that case you are challenged to manage the Jamaican traffic.

Using a seatbelt in a car and wearing a helmet when riding a motorcycle is required. Even when the use of a cell phone or texting is not explicitly forbidden, you should not do it. It is too distracting in the daily traffic, especially in the country side on winding roads.

As already mentioned, Jamaica has mountains and high, elevated plateaus, and the roads leading through this beautiful countryside are sometimes very winding. You are not familiar with the roads and don't know what is beyond the next curve. Therefore, a little tip: it is common in Jamaica to honk when you drive on these roads and when you have only a limited sight of the upcoming roadway.

Jamaicans are very communicative people, and they like to stop suddenly and chitchat at the road. Therefore, you must be very cautious when driving through the rural areas.

Besides the pedestrians, you have to look for route taxis. These are normal vehicles with a sign at the fender, and they stop frequently at the roadside to let people get in or get off.

Close to the capital of Jamaica, you have some toll roads, and you have to pay when traveling on these portions of the road. Therefore, always have cash with you. The toll depends on the length of your car and gets more expensive when your car is longer than 5.5 meters.

When you rent a car in Jamaica, you need a valid driver's license from your home country. You are allowed to drive with this license. However, when you stay for a period longer than six months, you should get a Jamaica driver's license.

As a driver of a rental car, you must often be at least twenty-three and not older than seventy-five years of age. When you don't meet the minimum age, you may be able to get a car; however, you have to pay a higher rate.

It is highly recommended to insure your vehicle with full coverage, to prevent liabilities in Jamaica. You should also know that the collision insurance that is normally included in your credit card benefits is not always accepted in Jamaica, and you have to pay collision separately.

If you feel uncomfortable to drive on your own, you can use a taxi service. The taxis are commonly sized cars, and they are regulated and controlled by the JUTA—Jamaican Union of Traveler Association. When you need a taxi, you call them, and a taxi will pick you up.

The taxi rates are calculated per car and not per passenger. When the taxi has a meter, then the price for the fare is determined by the meter. If not, you have to negotiate a flat fee for your trip with the taxi driver.

It is common to give the taxi driver a tip of 10 to 15 percent on top of the fare. The standard tip for taxi trips between midnight and five in morning is 25 percent.

Another transportation option is the local bus system in cities like Kingston. These buses connect the most important locations within the city limits.

Besides these buses, you also have an overland bus service. This service operates with smaller buses that stop whenever and wherever you want to get on or off. There are rarely fixed bus stop locations.

These small buses have a capacity of about twenty to thirty passengers, and they service the rural areas as well as the mountains.

The Jamaicans often use the route taxis to get from one point to another. These route taxis are serving the same roads like the buses; however, they are more flexible in their stops and in their route plans than the buses.

These taxis are normal passenger cars with a sign on the fender, and they are often fully occupied. These taxis stop frequently on their way; however, they let you pass and are helpful when you are lost on your way. We had this experience especially in rural areas, where we needed help to find the best way to our next travel stop.

The last option to travel is to walk or use a bicycle. However, Jamaica's roads are, even in Montego Bay or Ocho Rios, winding and steep; therefore, you need to be trained to use your bicycle in such areas. There are also no designated bike lanes, and you have to drive with the traffic.

While walking, you can adjust your steps and move slower and maybe have a little talk with other pedestrians or enjoy the surroundings or store windows.

When you are interested in exploring the plantations that are often higher in the mountains or the central plateau, it is often the best option to go with a tour company.

The roads to these still-operating plantations are often not marked with road signs, and they are not always open to the public. So it can happen that you make a private trip only to realize at the end that you are coming outside the opening hours.

When you need more information about this topic, you can reach us at the email at the end of this book.

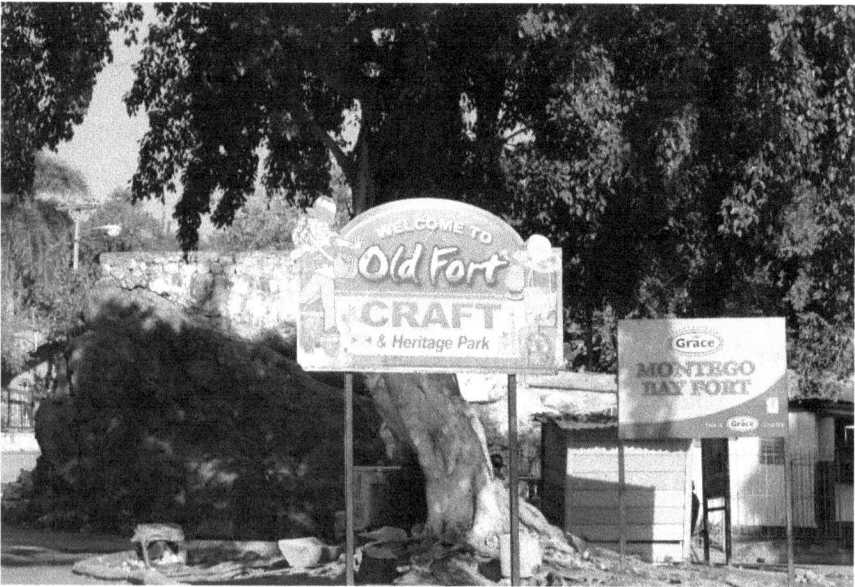

Attractions and Entertainment in Jamaica

Before you decide to reside and buy a property or start a business in Jamaica, you certainly want to know what else you will find here.

To give you an idea of what to expect, we put together a selection of events and important landmarks in the country. This will give you a clearer picture of the beauty of this tropical island.

Cultural Events

There are several interesting cultural events on Jamaica that you should know, so you can plan your trip. The following selection is limited because there are so many each month, and they are constantly changing, and new ones are added.

Jamaica is a country that has a wide range of cultural diversity to offer. They have artists that work in the painting and sculptural field. These artists combine the American-European art style with African techniques and colors. Internationally known artists like Dunkley Barrington or David Boxer are Jamaicans.

Dance and music is another field that is very popular in Jamaica. The music and dancing is strongly connected to their heritage from Africa, and you can distinguish three kinds of music: the interactive singing from the time of slavery, which was used for communication during the field work; the religious music with its drums and songs; and the dance music with its Caribbean rhythms.

For writers and authors, Jamaica is also a preferred location. One of the best-known authors is Ian Fleming who lived in Oracabessa at the northern coast of Jamaica where he wrote his famous James Bond stories.

Let's see how Jamaica celebrates their cultural community.

Arts and Crafts

Throughout the year, you will find many art and cultural events, where you can buy local paintings, sculptures, photography, and you can listen to the music. We describe a limited selection of these events; however, there are many more that you can visit.

One of these events is the Jamaica Jazz and Blues Festival in Priory. This event is in January and attracts celebrities beyond the Caribbean. In the past, artists like Celine Dion and Mariah Carey have participated in this event.

Every two years in June the Calabash Literary Festival takes place in Treasure Beach. This festival focuses on upcoming musicians, writers, and storytellers and offers them a stage for their art form.

The International Film Festival in Jamaica is in July each year and promotes the film industry in Jamaica. Local and international film professionals meet at this event, and musicians have the opportunity to experience the famous Tuff Gong recording studios. This is one of the most famous events in Jamaica and is also used by the city of Kingston as an opportunity to promote the wide cultural diversity of Jamaica internationally.

Food and Wine

There are several food festivals over the year. All these festivals celebrate the wide variety of the Jamaican cuisine. Jamaica's cuisine includes dishes from the native Arawak or Tainos as well as from the European, African, and Indian people.

In December there is the Milk River Seafood and Jerk Festival in Farquhar's Beach at the southern coast. This festival focuses on the local cuisine at its best.

In January Oracabessa celebrates its NyamJam Food and Music Festival. The location for this event is the Golden Eye Resort at the northern coast. Local and international chefs will pamper your taste buds, and local musicians give you the authentic and cultural Jamaican feeling.

In July each year, you can participate in the Port Antonio Jerk Festival. There you can try all kinds of jerked meat—chicken, pork, lobster, and much more. If you don't like meat, you will also find a selection of jerked vegetables, for example, roasted breadfruit.

You will discover at these events many interesting dishes and taste variations that tickle your taste buds and provide you with a wide range of culinary experiences.

Family and Fun Events

Throughout the year, there are several events where grown-ups and little ones have fun the same way.

In January there is the Accompong Maroon Festival in Accompong town. In this festival, the Maroons are celebrating their victory of the First Maroon War against the

British two centuries ago. At this festival, you learn interesting details about the Maroon heritage, their singing and dancing traditions as well as their food.

Another Maroon festival is in November and is called Misty Bliss. This festival focuses on the natural and historical heritage of the Maroon in the Blue and Crow Mountains.

The next family fun event is the Jamrock Summer 90 days of fun. This event is during mid-May and mid-August and consists of many smaller activities island-wide. These activities offer many fun events focused on sports, fashion shows, food, music, and much more. They are a welcomed distraction for the whole family during the hot summer time.

On August 6, Jamaica celebrates its political independence from the United Kingdom. Each year there are culturally inspired festivals, and this year this festival was called Proud and Free Jamaica 53. This fifty-third anniversary was celebrated in Jamaica for seven days starting on August 1. Look for next year's festival; it will certainly be as colorful and cheerful as this year's.

This is a limited selection of the events in Jamaica with the focus on family, fun, food, art, and craft. The sporting events are listed in the wellness and sport section of this book.

Museums and Historic Sites

The island of Jamaica was already inhabited for nearly a thousand years before the first European—to be exact, the Spaniards—set foot on the island in 1494. It is believed that this West Indies tribe named Tainos came from the northeast part of South America and settled on the island.

The Tainos called the island Xaymaca based on the natural resources that they found on their arrival: wood and water. Even today, Jamaica has big regions of forest, and in the mountain areas, you find many rivers and waterfalls that cascade over rocks and boulders.

About the time before the Spanish ships arrived, there were no written documents available. All known facts about the natives of Jamaica were gathered and documented by the Spaniards upon their arrival. There are also no historical sites from the Tainos left that you can visit.

The known and documented history of Jamaica started when the Spanish conquerors explored this undiscovered territory. They delivered reports to their superiors about their findings. Based on the findings of Columbus, this Caribbean island was not very interesting for the Spanish empire, because it was only interested in gold, silver, and precious stones, and none of this was found on Jamaica.

The Spaniards used Jamaica as a support base for their conquest on the American continent, and for that reason they constructed cities and ports along the coast. You can find at many places around the coastline historical buildings from the Spanish colonial time.

With the Treaty of Madrid in 1670, the British got Jamaica as an overseas possession, and the island became a part of the British Empire.

The British kept Spanish Town as the capital of the island until 1872 and moved the government in that year to today's capital, Kingston. Many of the historical sites from that time and until the independence in 1962 are located in Kingston.

In the following section, you will find a selection of the historical sites that demonstrate Jamaican history and further related attractions of interest throughout the island.

Spanish Town

The town is one of the oldest existing settlements in Jamaica, and it was the capital from the sixteenth to the nineteenth century.

Spanish Town was founded in 1534 under the name Santiago de la Vega, and when the British became the rulers of the island, it was renamed.

During the British attack in 1655, Spanish Town was damaged, and the British opened their administration at that time in Port Royal. When in 1692 an earthquake destroyed Port Royal, the government was moved back to Spanish Town, which was rebuilt in the meantime.

The government resided in Spanish Town until 1872 and then moved to Kingston, because all the economic and cultural life had already moved to the new capital.

There are still historical buildings in Spanish Town that give you the feeling of the colonial age. Next to the historical prison, which is still in use today, you will find the oldest Anglican church outside the United Kingdom.

A bit further down the street, you find Emancipation Square with its surrounding historical buildings. At the south side of the square is the old courthouse, and on the opposite side is the Rodney memorial. This memorial remembers the British admiral Rodney who protected the island against the French invasion. The memorial complex also houses the Archives with precious historical documents of the Jamaican history.

On the east side of the square is the council building. In this building resided the first assembly of Jamaica during the British rule. This building is still in use and serves as an office for the parish administration.

Across from the council building is the old King's House, which was the residence of the governors in the past. A fire destroyed this structure, and only the façade is left. Behind the façade is the People's Museum of Craft and Technology.

On your walk through these old streets, you will feel the breeze of Jamaica's history.

Devon House

This historical building is located in Kingston at the Hope Road and offers you a glimpse into the British colonial time.

It was built in 1891 for the first black millionaire of Jamaica—Georg Stiebel. He was a child of a black housekeeper and a German-Jewish merchant and made his money with his investment in gold mining in South America. With the gains from his investments, he bought fifty-one acres of land and built his home. This home was only one of his ninety-nine properties on the island.

The estate is today only eleven acres in the heart of Kingston. However, it is one of the important national monuments and a tourist attraction where you can enjoy the tropic life in the shade of the big canopies of trees.

The surrounding former household buildings house little shops with upscale items and restaurants, bakeries, and an ice cream shop.

When you purchase a ticket for a guided tour, you will get a coupon for the famous ice cream at that shop. You should enjoy this sweet treat in the tranquility of the garden.

Rose Hall

This historic site was built in 1770 by John Palmer and his wife, Rose. The Great House was the center of a 6,600-acre sugar plantation at the northern coastline twenty minutes east of Montego Bay.

When the former owners died, the grandnephew inherited the plantation and married in 1820 an English beauty named

Annie. What he did not know was that Annie had learned voodoo and black magic from her adoptive mother. When Annie got tired of her husband, she killed him and the two other husbands that followed the first one into her bed. She disposed of all three, and, it is told, their graves are below three palm trees at the beach.

According to the legend, she not only killed her husbands, but she also tortured her slave workers and her slave lovers, until her last slave lover killed her. The slaves at the plantation cursed Annie at her funeral, and today ghost sightings are reported from time to time, and temporary residents in the Great House have sometimes ghostly feelings inside several rooms.

The Great House was restored in the 1960s and is a museum today. A restaurant in the basement and the location is available for private functions like weddings.

If you like ghost stories, do not miss this national monument.

Port Royal

The last historical site in our selection is the old town of Port Royal. When you arrive there, old pirate stories will come into your mind, and that is exactly what this old fort represents.

Port Royal was the second biggest settlement besides Spanish Town on the island in the past. It was not only the base for the British administration but also the meeting point for pirates like Henry Morgan and Blackbeard Teach until the earthquake struck in 1692. That earthquake swallowed two thirds of the town.

The survivors of that earthquake moved to Kingston, which started to develop, and the British government to Spanish Town, which was rebuilt since the British conquest.

Port Royal became a military base for the British. You can visit the old military buildings and get historical details about the most important events of Port Royal.

One of strangest structures in Port Royal is the Giddy house. During the earthquake in 1907, this house sank partly into the ground. When you are standing in it today, you get a queasy feeling, and you have problems walking across it in a straight line.

This concludes the short list of the historic sites in Jamaica. It is intended to make you curious enough to discover the island's past on your own.

Natural Preserves

There are many natural treasures to explore on Jamaica. Here is a small seclect of attractions that you should not miss:

Beaches

One of the reasons for visitors to come to Jamaica are the beaches, and Jamaica has many of them. There are public beaches and private beach areas. They are everywhere around the island.

You will find beaches with white sand, and at the south coast are some beaches with the so-called black sand. These sandy beaches allow easy access into the water of the Caribbean Sea. At the rocky coves, the water access is a little bit harder, and you should use beach shoes.

The difference between the public beaches and the private beach clubs is the admission fee. To go into the beach clubs, you have to pay a small fee; however, you will find excellently maintained sandy beaches with amenities like showers and beach chairs and sun umbrellas. The Doctor's Cave Beach in Montego Bay and the James Bond Beach in Oracabessa are such private beaches with admission fees.

Castleton Botanic Gardens

Twenty miles north of Kingston in the mountains, you will find the Castleton Botanic Gardens. In 1862 the former Bath Botanic Garden was relocated close to the town of Castleton. The park is easy to find because the main road cuts directly through it. You only have to find a parking spot along the road side.

This garden has fifteen acres with beautiful tropical vegetation and a rocky river bed of a small river. Picnic areas and benches invite you for a rest.

In the park you will find more than one hundred and eighty different palm trees and more than four hundred tropical specimens. And the best of all, there is no admission for the visit.

YS Waterfalls

As an example of the many waterfalls throughout the island, we chose the YS Waterfalls. This park opened in 1992 and offers visitors all kinds of adventures.

You can walk and climb through the rain forest along the waterfall or swim in the bubbling and jumping water pools of the cascades. Swim shoes are strongly recommended, so that you do not slip. Do not be afraid, there are lifeguards on site.

When swimming in the waterfall pools is not exciting enough, you can climb to the top of the waterfalls and slide on the canopy ride over the waterfalls.

To relax from this much excitement, you can jump into the spring pool at the ground level. This pool is like a swimming pool. The water for this pool comes from an underground spring and is refreshingly cool. The pool is not deep, so that you can enjoy it even when you cannot swim.

This waterfall park is located on a former plantation for cane and a supplier for logwood export to Europe. But these plantation days are over, and today the plantation is a breeding ranch for Jamaica Red Poll cattle. On your ten-minute tractor ride to the waterfalls, you will pass calmly grazing cattle herds.

When you go to this park, do not forget your swimsuit and the swim shoes, so that you can try all that the park has to offer.

Fern Gully

Another natural treasure of Jamaica is Fern Gully. This nature preserve is at the northern coast near Ocho Rios, a tourist destination.

As the name Ocho Rios indicates, there are eight rivers in that region. One of the rivers went dry after an earthquake in

1907, and its riverbed was paved as a road. This road is today the A3 road,, which runs southward to Colgate and Kingston.

When you take this scenic trip, you will drive through a green tunnel formed by rainforest trees and ferns. While driving through this green tunnel, you cannot see the blue sky, and the sunshine is only twinkling through the dense tree tops.

When you open your car window, you will feel a nice cool breeze, while driving through this natural tropical treasure.

Green Grotto

This is a cave system at the main coastal road between Montego Bay and Ocho Rios, which has a long historic story to tell.

At the very beginning, this cave was a dwelling place for the Tainos, and during the Spanish and British era, it was a famous hiding spot for runaway slaves. They went deep into the darkness of the cave system and hid. In the deepest parts of the cave system, you find underground lakes that helped the slaves to survive.

During the British attack in 1655, this grotto was the hideout for the Spaniards before they could escape to Cuba.

According to the tour guide, the spacious entrance lobby of the cave was temporarily used as a nightclub before it became a tourist attraction. He also mentioned that one of the lakes in the cave was a film location in the James Bond film Live and Let Die.

Wellness and Sports

Jamaica is a sportive country, and residents enjoy sporting activities. The traditional sports in Jamaica are football—also known as soccer—cricket, athletics like sprinting, and netball—an early form of basketball.

Several Jamaican athletes participated in the Olympic Games over the years, and they were very successful. Some of the fastest sprinters in the world are from Jamaica.

However, you do not need to be a world-class athlete to compete in Jamaica's sports events like the Reggae Marathon or the Treasure Beach Off-Road Triathlon. You are always welcomed to participate.

In many resort hotels, you will find tennis courts and other exercise options. From January until April each year, it is polo season in Jamaica. These polo events are well known worldwide, and they attract participating teams from overseas.

When you are active in sports, you have to relax too. For relaxation, Jamaica offers various wellness facilities in the major tourist centers of Negril, Montego Bay, and Ocho Rios. And do not forget Kingston with its Eden Gardens, which is one of the newest government projects for the expansion of the tourism sector.

Diving

Like many other Caribbean islands, Jamaica offers warm waters with many diving spots around the island. The best-known places are in the tourist centers of Negril, Ocho Rios, and Montego Bay.

These spots are at the northern and western coasts. The coral reefs and tropical fish are waiting for your discovery. Especially at the northwest coast between Negril and Montego Bay, you have the opportunity to explore various coral formations and fish populations in different water depths, because in that region is the Cayman Drop.

As already mentioned in the geography chapter, Jamaica is located on the northern edge of the Caribbean plate, and beyond this plate edge is the Cayman Trough. This trench is nearly twenty-five thousand feet deep, and that makes it one of the deepest underwater spots in the world.

There are several other diving locations along the coast; however, the center of the diving sport is in the northwest coastal region.

Golf

The sport of golf came with the British to Jamaica, and there are twelve golf courses with eighteen holes on the island. The most golf courses are on the north coastal area close to the tourist region of Montego Bay.

These golf courses are often part of a resort community and close to the beaches. While you are playing, you have a beautiful view of the open water of the Caribbean Sea.

The other hot spot for golf courses is Kingston, the capital of the island.

Depending on the location, you have to expect big price differences for a golf round. The prices start with US$35 on a weekday and go up to US$175. It is a good idea to check with the golf club about the prices, because sometimes there are discounts available based on your playing time.

Boating

Like any other island nation, Jamaica welcomes boaters; however, it is not yet a hot spot. You do not need to have your own boat when you want to explore the waters around the island. There are many charter boats available that you can rent with or without a crew.

To find the right boat for your needs and your checkbook, here are some details to consider when making your decision.

The boats are categorized in three tiers or categories. The categories are only indicators for the quality and equipment of the boat, not for the service quality of the charter company.

The first tier contains the newest and most modern equipped boats with all the important and fun features for your comfort and safety. These boats are usually not older than four years, and they are the most expensive ones.

Boats that are older than four years are often sold to charter companies of the second category, and their charter price is lower. However, sometimes there are also newer boats available that don't have the full scale of equipment than the category one, and for that reason, these boats are in the second category.

When you come with your own boat, you have to go through customs first before you can dock at any marina. There are only a few official ports allowed for this purpose. You have to check with the immigration and customs to find out which harbor is the one for your entry.

For your entry into Jamaica, you will need several forms for customs. These documents are boat- and crew-related. When you are not from the United States, you may need a visa from the Jamaican government before you are allowed to enter a marina.

In case you are interested in further details, you can send us an email at the address at the end of the book.

Plantation Tours

As already mentioned in the history chapter, Jamaica was a crown colony of the United Kingdom. During that time, it had only agricultural industries. That meant the island produced sugar, bananas, coffee, and other tropical fruits for the British and had to import all other products that the population needed and did not manufacture.

These export products were cultivated on the many plantations throughout the island. A few of these plantations are still working today and offer visitor tours. At other plantations, you can stay for a few days and enjoy the plantation lifestyle. Some of the plantations are stripped down to the former great house of the plantation. These buildings house now restaurants and hotels.

Here is a short list of such plantations:

Appleton Plantation

One of the best-known plantations in Jamaica is the Appleton Estate. This plantation is located on the southern border of the cockpit country in Nassau Valley.

This estate is the oldest sugar plantation and distillery in Jamaica. It produces sugar and rum and has so since 1749. To get a firsthand impression about the sugar cultivation and rum distillery, you can book a bus tour to the estate.

On this tour you will not only see the manufacturing process, you also have the opportunity to taste the different sorts of rum and liquors. You can even try the best rum of the distillery—the fifty-year-old barrel-aged Appleton Estate rum. In case you prefer a sweet liqueur the rum with pineapple taste may be a nice alternative. However, you can try as much as you want, and if you are lucky, you will get a lunch too.

To get the best value from this tour, have a driver to bring you home.

Catachupa Croyton Plantation

Another interesting plantation is Catachupa Croyton. This plantation is located in the foothills of the Catachupa Mountains. This plantation is also the birthplace of one of the national heroes: Samuel Sharpe. He was the leader of the slave rebellion in 1831.

This plantation produces coffee and pineapple, and you can visit this plantation on three days of the week. The route to this plantation is not indicated with signs, like many other attractions; therefore, an organized bus tour is recommended.

When you arrive at the plantation, you will have a guided tour through the coffee groves and hear many interesting details about the coffee roasting.

Before you drive home, you are invited to a barbecue lunch with pineapple and fruit juices. As a dessert, you can nibble at a juicy sugarcane.

Good Hope Plantation

The biggest sugar plantation in Jamaica was Good Hope, which is located close to Falmouth on the northern coast in the mountains of the cockpit country.

This plantation was bought in 1774 by John Tharpe. On his plantations in the cockpit country and around Falmouth, he had three thousand slaves working in his sugar fields.

Besides the sugar plantations, he also owned several waterfront properties in nearby Falmouth. His townhouse in Falmouth still exists and today houses the tax administration office.

The sugar production ended in 1902, and today the plantation cultivates citrus fruits like ugli and ortanique, which are exported.

The former plantation buildings are converted into a hotel with adventure appeal and beautiful views into the cockpit county. When you want to swim in the Caribbean water, the shuttle bus will take you to the private beach within thirty minutes.

Green Castle Plantation

On the east coast south of Port Maria, you find the Green Castle Plantation in the mountains. This plantation produces sugar and bananas and concentrates its efforts on organic eco-farming.

This kind of farming already attracts researchers and students as well as ecologically interested tourists. The goal of eco-farming is sustainability and business opportunities in this industry sector for the whole community.

On the plantation is also the largest orchid farm of the Caribbean located that attracts visitors and researchers. For visitors who are looking for a secret retreat, the suites in the mountain house are an excellent place to hide.

The view from the patio toward the Caribbean Sea as well as the view toward the Blue Mountains is breathtaking, and it is definitely worthwhile to stay for a few days. To the beach and to the village, it is only a short walk, so you will not need a car.

Old Tavern Coffee Estate

The last plantation that we will introduce is the Old Tavern Coffee Estate a few miles north of Kingston in the Blue Mountains.

The owner of this plantation—the Twyman family—emigrated in 1958 from England and started their single-estate coffee business.

In a single-estate business, all production steps are executed by the one company. That means the coffee beans are grown, processed, roasted, packed, and marketed at the same location. Usually the coffee grower sells his production to a processing company. The Twyman family did not accept that and fought for their right to do everything in their business in court and won in 1997.

The coffee grows at the height of four thousand feet, and the fog in this height helps with the ripening process. The owner of this plantation replaces chemical fertilizers in the growing and manufacturing process as much as possible with organic, self-produced fertilizers.

You can visit this coffee estate with an appointment, because the work on the estate is mostly done by hand and the owner guides the tour and has to make arrangements for such a tour. At the end of the tour, you are invited to a tasting of the famous Blue Mountain Coffee and you should not miss that.

This concludes our short list of attractions; however, there is much more to see and to do. When you send us an email, we can certainly give you additional valuable details.

Eat, Drink, and Be Happy

Let us come to the most important part of life—food and drinks—and where you find them. The restaurant and bar scene is diverse, and you can choose various types of bars and restaurants.

In the tourist center, you often find open-air waterfront bars, where you can enjoy the sunset with a cool drink in your hand. Many of the bars and restaurants have also covered patios and indoor facilities for casual dining and partying.

Specialties in Jamaica are the steel drum grills and fruit stands at the roadsides. The steel drum grill vendors offer their dishes freshly prepared, and you can take it home or eat it at their cooking stand. However, there are rarely tables or chairs for your comfort.

The fruit vendors sell their products at the roadside too, and sometimes they are standing nearly in the middle of the road. They sell all kinds of fruits ready to eat or to take home.

The food in Jamaica has a large variety of cultural influences and tastes. You will find traditional dishes from the early natives of Jamaica, the Tainos, as well as food from the Spaniards, British, Africans, Chinese, and Indians. The Asian immigrants also brought crops from their home country to Jamaica, and today these crops are still growing, and they are integrated into the international flavor of the Jamaican cuisine.

The people from the various countries not only brought their traditional dishes with them, but also their cooking techniques, which are today melded with the Jamaican cooking tradition.

The Jamaican dishes consist mostly of seafood and meats like pork or goat and tropical fruits. The national dish in Jamaica is the ackee and saltfish and another specialty are the Jamaican patties. These patties are dumplings filled with hot, seasoned meat, and they are delicious snacks when you are on the road.

Specialty dishes that are influenced by other cultural nationalities are, for example, curry goat or fried dumpling and fried plantain (a sort of banana) as well as jerked meat and steamed cabbage. A famous side dish to nearly every meal is rice and peas. The peas are pigeon peas or kidney beans.

In case you do not know what jerk means, the meat or seafood is poked with seasoning before it is cooked or baked. During the cooking process, the spices give the dish the specific flavor of the seasoning mixture.

Fruit juices are the usual beverage with Jamaican food and do not forget the rum cocktails and other alcoholic mixed drinks like rum punch.

Another popular cooking tradition is the Rastafarian-influenced cuisine. In this kind of cooking, the dishes are prepared and cooked in a specific traditional way. The meals are mostly vegetarian and have to be naturally prepared. The ingredients have to be without any additives like food coloring. The usage of salt is also reduced to only a minimum or none. As meat, only poultry or fish is allowed, but no pork.

This concludes the overview about Jamaica and its culture, and now we start with the topic of how to buy real estate properties or invest in a business in this tropical paradise.

Real Estate and Investments in Jamaica

After the general overview about Jamaica, you know what to expect. Maybe you get the impression that Jamaica is only a tropical vacation spot. However, that is only one side of the coin.

This country has more benefits to offer than sun, water, beaches, and gorgeous mountains and countryside.

The potential of this country is not only in the tourism sector and its related businesses. Especially in the last years, Jamaica has worked very hard to better its hard economic situation and establish new income sources for its citizens. The positive impact of these measures are already noticeable; however, there is still much to do ahead, and the Jamaicans are determined to move forward on this positive path.

Let's take a look into today's national and economic situation and see how you can benefit from the potential of Jamaica and grow your business in Jamaica.

Government Today

Until 1962 Jamaica was a crown colony of the United Kingdom. When Jamaica became independent, it decided to stay in the Commonwealth of Nations. That means Jamaica is politically independent with its own government; however, the head of the nation is still the monarch of the United Kingdom.

To get a better understanding for this detail, let us look into the governmental structure.

The constitution for independence in 1962 was approved by the United Kingdom and came into force with the Jamaica Independence Act of 1962 of the United Kingdom parliament. Since that time, the amendments and changes to the constitution are the responsibility of the Jamaican people.

The legislature power of Jamaica is carried out by the house of representatives and the senate. Both houses can suggest bills, which have to be examined by each house separately and decided on. Such a bill will become law as soon as it passes the majority vote of both houses and the governor-general signs the bill.

There is one exception to the proposing of bills. Bills that are regarding the state budget and taxation can only be prepared by the house of representatives.

During this legislative process, the proposed bill has to go through several rounds of readings and decisions. In case the senate exercises its veto right, it can only delay a financial bill for one month and all other bills for six months.

Let's come back to the two houses of parliament in Jamaica.

The number of representatives in Jamaica is constitutionally limited to sixty members who are elected by the majority of votes in the separate election districts. The members are elected for five years.

The second house is the senate. The senate consists of twenty-one senators who are appointed from the majority party and the opposition.

The majority party is the political party that has won the election and forms the government for the country for the next five years. With the electoral victory comes the position of the prime minister and his cabinet as well as the nomination of thirteen of the twenty-one senators.

The prime minister is the leader of the government who initiates governmental policies and programs, gives directions, and controls the governmental activities.

He also forms the cabinets with ministers and secretaries. According to the constitution, the cabinet must have at least eleven ministers, and only four of the cabinet members are allowed to be senators. The other cabinet members are selected among the members of the house of representatives.

The minority party forms the opposition, and based on the constitution, this party selects their opposition leader. Besides this position, the opposition has the right to select eight senators.

The prime minister also nominates the chief justice, the president of the court of appeal and the three service commissions after the consultation with the opposition leader.

The three service commissions are the judicial service, the public service, and the police service commission, which appoint, promote, dismiss, and discipline public servants.

All the above-mentioned positions in the legislation have been appointed by the governor-general. However, the appointments of these parliament positions are always based on previous consultations with the majority and opposition party leaders.

The governor-general is the representative of the queen, who is the head of the state. He is appointed by the United

Kingdom, and he should have no affiliation to any of the political parties in Jamaica.

His responsibilities are opening of parliament, representing the queen at official occasions like honors and parades, appointing governmental officials, disciplining officers of the civil service, and performes the prerogative of mercy on behalf of the queen. The governor-general has his privy council of Jamaica that advises him about these tasks.

The governor-general as well as the six members of the privy council are appointed by the monarch after consultation with the prime minister.

As already described, there are many checks and balances in place to ensure that legislation, executive, and judiciary are properly separated; however, Jamaica has installed the position of the contractor general.

The function of the contractor general is to monitor and investigate the award of the government contracts and the contracting parties. His department also issues licenses and permits and implements processes for the control of the proper usage of these licenses and permits.

As you see, Jamaica is a parliamentary democracy, and your investment will be safe. Your investment will be a win-win for both sides. You can establish your investment venture in a safe environment and make money. And Jamaica has the opportunity to grow together with you and prosper.

Currency System

When the Tainos lived in Jamaica, there was no money, and the natives of the West Indies used gold only for decoration purposes. They exchanged what they needed among each other.

When the Spaniards came in 1494, that changed. The Spaniards brought glass beads, scissors, and mirrors as barter. Over time, Spanish silver coins became a valid currency in Jamaica. These coins were called reals, and they came from the Spanish mints in America.

During the seventeenth and eighteenth century, there were many different coins used in Jamaica because there were many ships and sailors from other European empires on their way through the Caribbean Sea, and they brought their money.

You could find French and Portuguese coins as well as British and Spanish currency coins. By 1681, the first currency exchange rates for all these currencies were established. The normal exchange rate for the currencies at that time was eight reals equal one dollar, and there were smaller valuations like two reals equal a quarter dollar and so on.

During that time, there were also copper coins in circulation; however, the Jamaican African population did accept these coins, and so England had to bring silver coins and later cupro-nickel coins to Jamaica. In 1840 the British currency system became Jamaica's currency, and the Spanish coins were demonetized.

The first official Jamaican banknote was printed in 1837 from the Bank of Jamaica (this is not today's banking institution). These banknotes could be cashed in British pounds, Spanish dollars, and local currency.

Over the years, many of the Jamaican banks failed or merged with newly established banks like the Barclay's Bank and Canadian Merchants Banks. These banks printed their own banknotes and distributed them.

To get order in all these different currencies, the Notes Law was passed in 1904, and that was the start of the Jamaican banknote printing.

The right to print banknotes went, in 1960, to the Bank of Jamaica. On January 31, 1968, the Jamaican government decided to change their currency to the decimal system and introduced new banknotes in September 1969.

Besides the system change, the banknotes were also completely redesigned. The queen, who was on the former banknotes and coins, was replaced by national heroes and national flowers and fauna on the front. On the back are national landmarks. The colors of the banknotes and the denominations were not changed.

The coin design was also changed in the conversion. The weight of the coins remained the same, but the fronts of the coins now have the coat of arms, and on the back are national symbols and heroes.

Today the banknotes have the following nominations, and you can get them at any ATM with a US debit card or a commonly accepted credit card:

J$50, J$100, J$500, J$1,000, and J$5,000.

As coins you will see the following denominations:

10c, 25c, J$1, J$5, J$10, and J$20.

When you get money at the ATM, please keep in mind how much you will need. Because when you leave Jamaica, you have to change it back to your home country currency, and the exchange rate fluctuates daily.

Economy of Jamaica

Jamaica struggled for decades with a low growth rate and high public debt. During the last thirty years, the growth rate was on average 1 percent annually. This slow economic growth gave the Jamaican population a hard time to increase their income level.

As already mentioned, the income that is generated in one of the most important industries of the country—the tourism—does not stay in Jamaica, because the generated income flows into the balance sheets of the multinational travel companies and hotels and is not reinvested in Jamaica.

To grow its income, reduce its country debts, and stabilize the economy, the Jamaican government has started extensive and ambitious reforms and programs. These programs should increase the growth conditions, boost the confidence in the country's economy, and provide employment opportunities for the population.

For the implementation of these reforms and programs, the Jamaican government gets national and international support, and there are already positive results visible. The economic growth for 2015/2016 is forecast to be nearly 2 percent, and that is twice the growth rate the country had until now. However, there is a long way to go because of social issues and an average unemployment rate of 13 percent in April 2015.

The international assistance comes from the World Bank and is supposed to help with agricultural, rural, and urban development. Education projects, infrastructural projects, as well as private-sector development assistance, small-scale enterprises, and telecommunication are also included in the development efforts.

The midterm goal of the government is the modernization of the public sector to increase the capacity and effectiveness, which should decrease the existing economic pressure.

To stimulate private investments in high-potential industry sectors, the government creates the necessary economic environment and offers incentives. The primary goal is to create new jobs and shrink the unemployment rate, especially for the young population.

With education programs, the government grows a skilled workforce for these new, high-potential industry sectors. This education is not limited to the technology, digital, and animation projects for the young adults. Environmental and social projects are also part of this development strategy to strengthen the communities and motivate them to tackle their social issues.

Let's have a look into the existing industry sectors.

Tourism in Jamaica

Jamaica was always a tourist destination, and, according to the government data, the year 2015 was so far very successful. During the first nine months, the tourist numbers increased by 1.6 million—that is a growth of 5½ percent in comparison to 2014.

The number of cruise-ship visitors also increased by 105,000. Most of these visitors are from the United States and the United Kingdom.

For the coming winter season, an additional 60,000 flight passengers are expected, and more than 80 percent will come from the United States. For the next year, there is a nonstop connection between Dublin/Ireland to Montego Bay in the planning.

To accommodate all these new visitors, there are two new five-star hotels planned in the Montego Bay area.

Not only the lifestyle tourism is promoted by the government, the health tourism is the focus too. In Rose Hall is a twenty-two inpatient facility with two operating rooms and one delivery room as well as an outpatient portion scheduled.

Jamaica is on its way to becoming one of the leading tourism destinations in the Caribbean islands.

Agriculture in Jamaica

Another very important industry in Jamaica is the agricultural sector, which includes not only the growing of the crops and fruits, but also the packing and processing from the producer to the consumer.

In the past, Jamaica imported food from other countries. To become independent from these imports, the government started modernization projects in this part of the economy and implemented their drought-mitigation strategy. With these changes, it was already possible to increase the outcome of the agricultural production.

The positive results help Jamaica to be more independent from imports and sell their homegrown products on the local market and to local businesses like hotels and restaurants. In this case the country not only saves money but also generates internal income for its citizens.

Besides the agricultural production for the local market, Jamaica also produces for export. The exported items are sugar and rum as well as bananas, coffee, and cocoa.

New Targeted Industries for Growth

Besides the above-mentioned industries—tourism and agriculture—Jamaica also is an exporter for bauxite-alumina; however, this industry sector is not sufficient enough to offer and guarantee increasing employment and income for the population.

Therefore, the government has streamlined their business process to attract more foreign investments that will help to improve and provide sustainable economic growth for Jamaica and generate jobs for the population.

The country has education programs implemented for their young population in the digital and IT industry. With this growing, skilled workforce, the government wants to attract companies in the digital media sector and the animation production business.

Another economic sector that is booming and welcomed in Jamaica is business process outsourcing. These outsourcing processes can be call centers for products or services or assembly lines for products.

Based on its geographic location in the middle of the Caribbean Sea, Jamaica is also on its way to becoming a global transportation hub. Recently the government signed a contract that makes Jamaica the hub for liquefied natural gas in the Caribbean, and last year China contracted Jamaica as its distribution hub.

These are only a few opportunities that are available in Jamaica, and there is much more to explore. When you are interested to do business in Jamaica, let us talk about it. We can help you get started. Our email address is at the end of this book.

The Banking System in Jamaica

As already explained in the chapter on currency, there were many different kinds of currency in Jamaica. They were controlled by the currency board system in the past. With the independence, it was necessary to form a central bank institution for the new nation, and in 1960 the Bank of Jamaica was formed based on the Bank of Jamaica Law. With the establishment of this central bank, the former currency board system was ended and replaced.

The Bank of Jamaica is the supervising banking institution for all deposit-taking institutions in the country and provides a payment system for the connected institutions. Remittance companies and exchange trades are also regarded as deposit-taking institutions.

The main objectives of the Bank of Jamaica are to issue and to redeem banknotes and coins. This bank also keeps and administrates the reserves of Jamaica and influences the volume and the conditions for the available credit in the supervised bank institution. As the banking institution for the government, the Bank of Jamaica is also the banking institution for the government, and it monitors and influences the money and capital market with its financial regulations.

Let's have a look into the banking scene.

There are currently six deposit-taking institutions licensed in Jamaica, and their license gives them the right to buy, sell, and deal with foreign currency, take deposits, and provide loans to foreign nationals. Citibank and Bank of Nova Scotia are two of these banks.

Beside the above-mentioned institutions, there are the merchant banks and building societies. These are specialized banking institutions, which have restrictions in their business scope.

Credit unions are not yet introduced to the financial market in Jamaica, because the governmental regulations for the introduction of these financial servicers are not yet finalized and in place.

For the currency exchange business, there are several specialized companies in the market. You find many of them in airports or ports and inside of shopping malls. The purpose of such a company is to take your foreign currency and exchange it into Jamaican dollars based on the daily fluctuating rate. These companies also facilitate the international money transfer from or to Jamaica. They are Cambios and Bureau de Change or remittance companies.

To use one of these services, you have to be prepared to present documents showing who you are and where your money comes from. The documentation depends on your service request.

Besides the above-mentioned deposit-taking financial institutions, there are also nondeposit-taking financial institutions. Examples for the latter are insurance, mutual funds, or pension funds. These financial services companies are regulated and supervised by the Financial Service Commission and not by the Bank of Jamaica.

Taxation in Jamaica

Yes, Jamaica has taxes, and everybody who earns income in Jamaica has to pay his or her fair share. Nonresidents and foreign nationals are not excluded, and the government of Jamaica is working with your home country in one or another way.

For example, between the United States and Jamaica exists an information exchange agreement, and between several other states exists a tax withholding agreement. Therefore, when you are earning interest, dividends, or any other income in Jamaica, it is a good idea to have an accountant to help you through the tax laws in Jamaica and your home country. There are also strict deadlines for the payment of taxes due in Jamaica, and penalties apply shortly after the expiration of such a deadline.

In some cases, legal documents become void when you do not pay the attached tax or duty amount. Therefore, be very careful in this matter.

All tax-liable individual will need a taxpayer registration number—short TRN—and this number is your tax identification for your annual tax filing. The deadline for your tax filing is March 15 every year, and that is two weeks before the country's budget year starts.

The tax filings are mandatory when you are employed and if you earn any additional income from self-employment or interests and dividends. When you are employed, your employer pays the income taxes from your monthly salary; however, the income taxes for your self-employment is due quarterly, and you have to pay this tax portion yourself.

When you fail to file your taxes, the tax authority will estimate your taxes and will add a penalty right away.

There is a tax-free income threshold for Jamaicans. This threshold does not apply for nonresidents. The income tax rate for nonresident individuals is 25 percent in Jamaica. There may be a tax rate due in your home country, and to find out the best tax option for your individual situation, you will need the advice of a tax expert.

You can pay your taxes either online—that option was recently introduced—or you have to go to one of the twenty-nine different local tax offices throughout the island. Besides the individual income taxes, there are other types of taxes that may or may not apply to your individual situation.

When you only live short-term in Jamaica and stay in a hotel, you have to pay accommodation tax and general consumption tax.

The accommodation tax will be charged and paid by the hotel or the landlord where you stay during your visit in Jamaica. This tax is calculated per room and night and starts with US$1. You will find this amount on your accommodation bill.

The general consumption tax is a value-added tax and is calculated on each stage of the production or distribution level for goods and services. This tax is usually 16½ percent; however, there are some different percentages for products in the telecommunication sector and tourism. This tax is due as soon as the business passes the exemption threshold, and the business owner is responsible for this tax.

When you own a house or condominium or a commercial property in Jamaica, there are annual property taxes to pay. The property tax is calculated on the market value of the unimproved land; the structures on the land do not influence the tax amount.

The land value is defined by size, zoning, land type, development potential, and much more. The total land value determines the percentage for the tax calculation. For land value below the threshold, you have to pay a fixed amount of J$1,000. For the excessive amount of the unimproved land value, the tax rate is 1½ percent, according to the tax information. The calculated tax amount is due on April 1 each year.

The paid taxes are used for the maintenance and expansion of street lighting, collection and disposal of solid waste, community infrastructure and civil improvements, repair of fire stations and farm roads as well as the local administration.

When transferring a property, there is a property transfer stamp duty due. The amount of this duty is calculated on the market value of the property and is paid by the seller. The transfer of a property is only legally binding when all taxes and stamp duty are paid; otherwise, the documents get void after the deadline for the payment.

There is no capital gain tax in connection with real estate sales in Jamaica. When you use the property as an investment property and collect rent, you have to pay income tax for your rental income, and you have to charge the consumption tax for the monthly rent.

The tax offices are also in charge of issuing driver's licenses and all car-related alterations and changes. Necessary business licenses and permits are handled by this government department too.

Many documents in real estate and business need to be stamped and notarized, and this task is also done in the tax offices. Each stamp action has its fees attached, and there are different deadlines for the payments. To avoid problems and penalties, you should pay these amounts immediately when they occur.

How to Do Business in Jamaica

After many year of hard struggles with debts and rising credit levels, Jamaica takes all efforts to make their economy thrive and to attract new businesses and investments from foreign countries.

The biggest problems for investors and businesses were the hurdles during the start-up phase and the operation of a business. The process was hard to follow through and was very time consuming.

During the last year, the government introduced a new initiative, which has improved these processes dramatically. The government has synchronized the national quality requirements and standardized their framework in this field. That has bettered their country's position for the goods and services on the global trade stage.

The government has also encouraged their own population to expect and demand more quality from their own local producers, manufacturers, and service providers. This demand was not only addressed to the big players but also to small and middle-sized companies and made them more competitive on the global market.

These efforts already opened and boosted many opportunities for new markets, new market participants, and global investors. Jamaica has improved its position and is today one of the top ten most improved countries globally.

Besides the stimulus for trade and export, the government also pushed for better and higher education to make the country interesting for international businesses that look for process outsourcing opportunities.

The port authorities in Jamaica are actively promoting their logistic and freight services and have already succeeded in becoming the main hub for China products to the Americas. Jamaica is also the hub for liquefied natural gas in the Caribbean.

Two important industries with homegrown products besides agriculture are the bamboo furniture industry and the strongly regulated and licensed ganga cultivation and distribution for medical and religious purposes.

After this short discourse, let us see how you can participate and get into the Jamaican market. It is easier now than it was in the past.

The government offers many different kinds of incentives to attract global investments—big or small. The incentives start with employment and tax relief for all business types and income tax relief for large-scale and pioneer industries.

There are several different reduced customs duty tariffs for core industries, especially for raw materials, production, and manufacturing businesses in the Jamaican free zones. For real estate developers, the government also offers tax reductions and exceptions for certain development projects.

This information should always be verified when you make your business decisions and when you actually start your business, because such incentives can change or be modified.

Before you start, you need to know your business goal and how you would like to operate your business in Jamaica, because these decisions will impact your path through the governmental process.

You can operate your business as a company or as a sole-trade or a partnership. Based on your business decision, you have to contact different governmental entities and register your business.

With this registration information, your way leads you to the tax authority and insurance agency, which are mandatory before you can start your business operation. When you have accomplished all registrations, you should get a tax certification, which is proof for the successful opening of your business.

In case you are a developer, you have to connect with several agencies in this industry sector such as the environmental and building departments. These are only examples. When you want assistance, send us an email with your question.

When you open a business and you hire employees, you also need to know the legal and social requirements for employment. There are working permits necessary for foreign nationals, and there are minimum wage and vacation time requirements to keep in mind.

Your business opportunity in Jamaica can be very beneficial for you, when you start it correctly. The success is right in front of you when you enjoy life in one of the richest cultural areas and happiest countries of the world.

Living and Working in Jamaica

Jamaica is a country that is named in several international studies as a country with a high quality of life based on life expectancy, literacy, education, and standard of living. It is also in fortieth place on the happiest countries list, and the criteria for this valuation are the low ecological footprints, the rich culture, as well as the social and physical infrastructure.

Details and examples of these criteria we have already described in the previous chapters, and that makes Jamaica one of the most attractive islands in the Caribbean.

When you intend to stay only for a short period of time in Jamaica, you often can arrive without a visa with your passport. However, before you start your trip, you have to check if that applies for your home country.

There are three different options that can apply. Either you are coming from a country that does not require a visa, or you will get the visa at the port of entry, or you have to get the visa before your arrival in Jamaica.

Citizens from countries like Germany do not need to have a visa. They can arrive in Jamaica with the following documents, and they will not experience any problems.

The passport must have a picture und must be valid at least for the period of the stay. Furthermore, you need your return ticket and a statement about sufficient funds for your stay, and you should not be on a crime watch list.

When you are coming from a country with illnesses like dengue fever, you will need to provide proper health documentation showing that your vaccination is current.

In the above case, you will either get permission to stay for thirty or ninety days—whatever the immigration officer allows you.

When you have the above-mentioned documentation, but you are coming from a country that requires a visa, you have to check if you can get your visa at the port of entry or if you have to apply for your visa in the Jamaican Embassy in your home country before you start your journey.

The above-mentioned criteria are mandatory for all visitors and tourists. When you want to stay longer and intend to work or to do business in Jamaica, then be prepared for additional paperwork.

In case you want to work in Jamaica, you must definitely have a job offer with a local employer before you come to Jamaica and apply for a work permit. You are not allowed to work before your application is processed and granted. The only exception from this process is either a diplomatic status or when you are married to a Jamaican citizen.

The definition of work includes every kind of employment with the purpose to gain income from it, and it does not matter if this employment is voluntary, commercial, business, professional, charitable, or entertainment.

The application for a work permit includes a questionnaire with more than fifty questions, which need to be answered by you and your employer. In this questionnaire, your employer has to explain why you are the person for the offered job and not a Jamaican. The employer also has to prove what efforts he or she had done to find the best matching employee for that specific job in Jamaica.

Besides the questionnaire, there are several other documents necessary for this process like your resume, certified copies of your professional qualifications, recommendations and reference letters, police report from your home country, to note only a few.

This work application process costs J$14,000 once non-refundable and J$108,000 annually for the renewal fee. These fees can be paid either by you or your employer. The amount can change, and it is based on the available information in November 2015.

In case you intend to stay for the rest of your life in Jamaica and want to get permanent residency, then you need to be a little bit more patient, because that process can take up to three years.

The permanent residency has a few additional documentary requirements before it is granted. You have to establish your financial situation and the capability to support yourself for a long period of time. You also have to pass a medical exam.

Besides the common personal documents like a birth certificate or marriage papers, you also need a criminal background check from the Jamaican police and at least two local reference statements from reputable Jamaican citizens.

To get the local reference papers, you need to establish a good relationship with your local references before they will be willing to help you with this task. These local references also have to accept visits from the police or the immigration authorities, because they will verify the given information about you. Such a process takes time, and that is the reason why you need patience.

The application fee for this process is J$30,000 non-refundable, and because of the importance of such immigration documents, it is best to deliver the papers in person at the immigration office.

Maybe the above information will make you think twice, but do not hesitate. Go to Jamaica and explore the country for yourself and make up your mind while you are there.

There were many important and celebrity residents in Jamaica before you, and they all loved the country. They were film stars, singers, writers, and artists that left their footprints on the island.

When you need assistance getting started, we are happy to help. Send an email to the address at the end of this book.

Let us now begin with a few other interesting secrets of Jamaica: the real estate opportunities.

A Home in Tropical Jamaica

The island of Jamaica is the third largest island in the Caribbean, and it is after very hard financial struggles over the last decades on an economically improving path. The economy is growing, and the government makes every effort to attract business investments for their country. These investments can either be from visitors or from businesspeople who come, stay, and start a business.

How the government is presenting Jamaica to the potential business community, we have already described. Let us now look at what the country offers in the real estate sector and what you need to know when starting your investment in real estate.

Development investments into the housing market are welcomed from businesspeople as well as from individuals who look for a vacation or second home on the sunny, tropical island of Jamaica.

From Miami in Florida, it is only a short flight of ninety minutes to Kingston or Montego Bay, and many air carriers have excellent flights routes. For the Canadians as well as for the Europeans from the United Kingdom or Germany, Jamaica is one of the preferred vacation retreats, and it is easy and affordable to purchase a condominium or a house in this tropical paradise as a second home.

The majority of the population (more than 1.6 million) live in Kingston, Spanish Town, and in the surrounding areas. Montego Bay, the second largest population center, is home to about 82,000 people and the rest—1,203,000—occupy the smaller towns, the mountain regions, and the plateaus.

To get an impression what to expect from the different areas on Jamaica, here are a few details about the regions and the real estate inventory. The presented numbers are only a limited selection of the properties, and they are used to demonstrate the price ranges in the market.

For detailed information of your target area, please contact us. It will be our pleasure to assist you with your real estate project in Jamaica.

Kingston

Kingston is the capital and the business center of Jamaica. It is the biggest town with about 1.5 million residents. The city consists of Kingston, which is the old downtown area and New Kingston (please note: Spanish Town is not included).

The Kingston area includes the harbor and the island with Port Royal and the Manley International Airport. The commercial areas are close to the port and the airport.

The governmental departments and agencies are located in Kingston as well as the main educational institutions and universities.

In the historical part of Kingston, there are mostly two- to three-story buildings. These houses are of older construction. The most parts of the city are low-level buildings; however, there are more and more high-rises constructed. These high-rises are either offices or business towers or hotels. Many of the business towers are close to the harbor and waterfront in Kingston.

There are also many tourist attractions in the city like the Devon House or the Emancipation Park or the Bob Marley Museum, to name only a few. To visit these attractions or to move around in the city, you can use the public buses or take a taxi.

The residential areas with single-family homes are outside the busy downtown area. These homes are mostly one- or two-story buildings on a fenced lot.

When you move more into the mountains, you will find more gated communities with two-story, single-family homes and condominiums. These condominium complexes are often only three or four stories. Sometimes these condos are constructed into the rock, and so they have an unobstructed view to the downtown area of Kingston.

You will find single-family homes in various price ranges in Kingston as well as condominiums. The prices vary based on the conditions of the property and the location. Many of these homes are also available for rent.

Listing prices for single-family homes start at US$23,000 up to US$3,250,000. For a condominium, you have to pay at least US$29,400, and the highest price is about US$700,000.

As rent, you can calculate US$2 per square foot, and the rental properties in Kingston start at US$303, and for a two-story mansion, your rent would be US$10,000 monthly. (We use US dollars for this information, because the amounts are more readable than the J$ dollar amount.)

Montego Bay

The second largest city in size and the fourth biggest city in population is Montego Bay at the northwest coast of the island. This town was in a former time a port for leather and beef. Today Montego Bay is one of the tourist centers.

Montego Bay has the largest international airport in Jamaica and is a tourist hub. The most flight connections are between Jamaica and the United States, United Kingdom, Canada, and Germany.

The city is located at the shore of a bay with smooth surrounding mountains. The hotels and resorts are conveniently built close to the beaches like Doctor's Cave Beach. Many tourist attractions and activities like Rose Hall are close by. Cities like Negril and Falmouth are also not far away and can be reached easily by car.

The buildings in the downtown and historical center are mostly two- to three-story buildings with apartments on the second floor and businesses on the first. The single-family homes are one story or two stories. They are fenced and often have a patio on the second floor.

Because of the surrounding mountains, much new residential construction is along and up the hillside. That gives many homes a terrific view to the open sea and beautiful sunsets.

When your home is on the hillside and close to the downtown and shopping centers, you can easily walk from one place to the other. There are small stairways and elevators down the mountains toward the main road.

The price range for a single-family home in Montego Bay varies between US$30,250 and US$1,662,985, while you can get a condominium in that area for about US$50,000 and up.

Ocho Rios

Another main tourist spot in Jamaica is Ocho Rios. It is best-known for its resorts and the entertainment at the beach. In the port, not only cruise ships anchor, but also cargo ships are loading their cargo like bauxite from a nearby mine.

In that region are tourist attractions like the Green Grotto, the Dunn River Park to the west, and Oracabessa with its James Bond beach and the former villa of the writer Ian Fleming to the east. His villa is today the Golden Eye Hotel and Resort.

A little hint for James Bond fans: parts of the James Bond film Dr. No were filmed in Ocho Rios and in the surrounding areas. Another famous James Bond film spot is the Green Grotto.

The area around Ocho Rios is more flat, and therefore fewer residential properties are glued to the mountainside. The majority of the residential buildings are single-family homes with a fenced backyard.

The homes in Ocho Rios are between US$69,000 and US$590,000, and for only US$26,900, you can be a proud condominium owner in this town.

Beyond the Tourist Centers

Besides the tourist and business cities, there are many middle-sized and small towns throughout the island that hold many interesting real estate opportunities for you.

These regions are for people who love the tranquility, fresh air, and beautiful countryside. The houses are often located in the mountains and can be reached by community roads.

Because of the limited flat land, these properties are single-family homes that are built in the height, and they usually have an unobstructed view into the tropical mountain vegetation.

The prices in this area are below the above-mentioned prices; however, the prices in that region are varying, and the advice of a local real estate professional is essential to find the right property of your dreams.

Real Estate Market Data in November 2015

During our stay in Jamaica, we experienced that there are many vacant land offerings and new construction going on, and some of the construction projects are nearly finished.

In many areas on the island, we saw properties that were still in the construction phase, and the first floor is already occupied. Our research showed that there are many reasons for this. Many owners started their project of a new home with their own money and their sweat money (please note: sweat money means the muscle power and skill that you as the homeowner put into your home project). The sweat money is available as long as they are able to move; however, the cash is the problem.

The owners need money to buy supplies like bricks, sand, cement, and wood. Later in the process, they need professionals for plumbing and electrical, and these professionals cost cash money too.

The lack of experience in the planning of such a huge project and sometimes the overpriced services or underestimated expenses of professionals result in a financial shortfall for the homeowner. The homeowner deals with this shortfall by putting the project on hold and finishing the rooms that are already constructed and moves in. The rest of the house will be finished as soon as there is more cash available.

Such a building process is and was possible, because the regulations in Jamaica in regard to permits and licenses are not very strict. However, the government is improving this process and will certainly enforce the process in the future. With these changes, not only will the real estate sector win, but also the overall economy, because it will create job opportunities for the population.

Another reason why the construction stopped at many houses is that the owner often does not want to apply for a mortgage for his building project. There are trust issues with authorities involved like providing much personal and family information during the mortgage application process.

Furthermore, the pieces of land are registered with the state for tax purposes, and the government guarantees the title; however, many owners often do not have the original title document to present to the lending institution. To get this title document involves a process with many documentation requirements and waiting times until the certificate of title is issued. For the mortgage application, this certificate of title is a mandatory document.

Besides the private construction and individual home-building projects, there are also the new construction developments throughout the island. Some of these developments are supported with government grants to provide affordable housing for a growing number of new homeowners.

The second and vacation home development in the tourist centers are an additional opportunity for Jamaica to attract foreign investments and generate income for the state.

When you are interested in getting more information about the Jamaican real estate market and how to get successfully started in this investment sector, please send us an email at the address at the end of the book.

For the real estate market, the Realtor Association of Jamaica provides a Multiple Listing Service for their members; however, this MLS is not available to the public user. That means that on each association member's website, you will only see the properties that are under an exclusive listing contract with the website owner.

With the entering of the exclusive listings into the MLS, these listings are transferred to the international website of the NAR-National Association of Realtors in the United States. On this international website, there are the listings from the Jamaica MLS with limited details to the properties.

The research on this real estate database for Jamaican properties showed in November 2015 the following property figures:

Total listings 2,502, thirty-five of these listings could not be verified if they are rentals, commercial or residential, because of missing specifications in the database.

Homes   1,592   US$14,189   to US$6,215,953

Condos   are not verifiable on that database.

Land   875   US$6,677   to US$79,813,056

Commercial properties   are not verifiable on that database.

As you see, there are many land lots on the market, and these pieces of land are all over the island. However, the square-foot prices and size of the lots vary strongly in the different areas.

To give you an idea how many properties from the above-mentioned total numbers are listed by one real estate office, here is the breakdown:

Homes	354	US$23,000	to US$3,250,000
Condos	340	US$29,400	to US$685,000
Land	150	US$7,984	to US$1,500,000
Commercial	100	US$21,008	to US$3,023,445

As these numbers demonstrate, you can get started in your dream home hunt on an international property website. But the information that you will find there gives you only a small hint what is available and how much such a property may cost you. For details you definitely have to consult a real estate professional to get exactly your dream home.

When you make your decision about what kind of property you want to acquire, please keep in mind that a newly constructed home may be a better option for you, because the home is built based on the actual building code, and it often includes energy-efficient features that will save you money in the long run.

The properties in such a development are government regulated, because each landowner who wants to provide six or more units on the land has to be registered with the state and needs to provide many documents for the development project. During the development period, the government can inspect and control the development processes and financials, so that your investment in such a development is protected.

Older homes are often not up-to-date and need improvements on the interior as well as in energy-saving measures. The updates of energy-saving features are always a good idea, because of the tropical climate. Based on the traditional home construction, you may need to make some adjustments to the exterior structure—for example, new windows. This change keeps the warm air out, the cold air inside, and that will save you money with your electric bill.

Now let's have a look into the rental market. It does not always make sense to buy a property, and in such a case, a lease is a better option.

When you are looking for rentals, you first have to decide if this is a commercial rental if you would like to open a business or if you need a place because you are on the house hunt for your dream home.

When leasing a commercial place, you have to focus your search based on your business purpose. When you need, for example, a shop for the sale of your products, you should look for a place in a mall; otherwise, an office building is a better choice when you offer services.

Here is a little lease price information for your business project from one real estate office website for the location in Kingston:

You can get a small business place for US$252 monthly up to US$42,666 monthly and the average square-foot price is US$5.

The rental price for a private apartment starts at US$303 and goes up to US$10,000 per month. In this case the square-foot price is US$2.

Please let us know when you need more details for your future business or private property venture in Jamaica. We can get you what you need.

General Information about Real Estate in Jamaica

When you are looking to invest in real estate in Jamaica, you are in the right place. A home on this tropical island has many benefits for you.

You can purchase a home on the island, even when you are not a citizen of Jamaica. There are no restrictions on home ownership. You can do whatever you want with your property. You can use it, sell it, or rent it.

There are some details to know when owning a property. You will have to pay annual property tax and income tax when you rent your property. The annual property tax is assessed each year on the market value of the unimproved land, and the income tax is based on the income earned during the tax year. For each monthly rent payment, you have to collect a general consumption tax from your tenant. You have to forward this tax to your tax offices within thirty days when it is paid by your tenant.

When you sell your property, you have to pay your share of the closing costs, which includes the transfer tax. This transfer tax applies also when inheriting a property. Besides the Jamaican tax rules, you also have to consider the tax implications from your home country.

Only 55 percent of all property pieces in Jamaica are properly registered, and therefore you have to do your due diligence when you acquire a property. The property transfers may be recorded; however, this recording does not necessarily include a registration of the current owner.

To address this issue, the government has started a program for the land registration. When the land is not registered to the current owner, he or she cannot use this land for any financing purposes like getting a mortgage. Therefore, this program is a good opportunity to get the land registry records up-to-date, and for you as a buyer, it is easier to evaluate who is the owner.

The registration of the land is voluntary. However, it is always a problem when you buy a property that is not properly registered to the current owner. Before you make an offer on a property, you should investigate who is the owner. In case the owner is not registered for the property, he or she must be able to prove the ownership of the land with reliable documents.

It is possible for every property owner to register his or her land parcel. For this registration, the existing owner needs to have proof about his or her purchase of the land, his or her ID, and at least two reputable people who can testify about the title's history for at least thirteen years. These are only the most important details for a land title, and there are some more details to evaluate before the registration process can be completed and the certificate of title is issued to the parcel owner.

There is no title insurance necessary in Jamaica because the government of Jamaica guarantees every title to a piece of land. It is also mandatory that the property transfer process is done by attorneys—the attorney of the buyer and the attorney of the seller—and that insures that your buyer's interests are represented and that you get a clean title for your property.

Before you make an offer on a specific property, you should have at least investigate the title of the property, so that you make your offer to the correct seller. When the seller is interested in selling the property to you, he or she will retain an attorney who will draft the sale contract based on the seller's conditions.

You will get the drafted sale contract, and you should hire your own attorney who reviews and represents you in the transaction to protect your interests in the transaction. Realtors in Jamaica are not allowed to prepare the contracts; they only bring buyer and seller together.

When both sides—seller and buyer—have signed the contract, it is binding. The buyer has to make his or her first portion of the purchase price as earnest money. Usually 10 percent plus an additional amount for arising closing costs are sufficient. The balance of the purchase price is due at the closing table.

For each transfer of a real estate property, you have to pay stamp duty and transfer tax as well as other transaction expenses. The detailed expenses are described in the chapter Purchase Statement for the Transaction.

When you buy a piece of land to build your own home, you are more flexible in getting what you want. You make your own plans for your home, and the contractor builds your dream house accordingly to your wishes. Further information on this topic you find in the chapter Building Your Dream Home in Jamaica.

Property Details in Jamaica

In the previous chapter, you got general information about real estate. Let us now take a look into property construction.

In Jamaica you will find different construction styles in the existing housing inventory. The traditional Jamaican home is called Jamaica vernacular, and these houses are mostly older construction. The house is small and has a rectangular shape with a higher pitched roof. Some of these houses have nice verandas, and they are often made of wood. The higher roof also kept the interior of the house cool, because the hot air moved to the ceiling.

The newer built homes often have the same traditional shape; however, they are mostly bigger, constructed with stone, sand, and cement, and they often have a second floor.

Another interesting feature in many houses is the patio. It is often on the second floor. This patio is enclosed by a decorative wrought-iron grating. The lot around the house is usually fenced.

In some houses, there are no glass windows, only windows with plantation shutters. When you open these shutters, the air can flow through the house, and the moisture from inside the house is blown outside. In newer construction, there are inside air-conditioning units in each room, and you can cool each room separately. Central air systems are not seen very often.

The water heater is often put onto the roof of the building, and you can recognize it as a big, bulky, black block. The electricity is not standardized everywhere; therefore, you either find 110 or 220 volt.

Usually the cars are parked in the fenced yard, because there are not that many houses with a garage. Newer constructed houses and higher priced homes have at least a one-car garage.

In some yards you will find trees and shrubbery; however, the lots around the houses are small, and there is not much room for lush landscaping.

Private pools are not standard in private homes in Jamaica. Such a feature is a luxury and will take valuable space from the yard that can be used much more efficiently.

Condominium complexes are often fewer than four stories high, and often they have only two stories and no elevators. However, in the newer constructed condominium complex, high-rise buildings come more and more into fashion to use the land more effectively.

Besides the traditional house style, you will also find all kinds of housing styles that the former empires brought with them during their period of reign.

You will find the Spanish-inspired houses with an enclosed backyard from the colonial time; however, this style is modernized to today's taste.

Another style is the British colonial style. These houses are two-story buildings with covered verandas around the house, and they give you an airy feeling with their outdoor design.

When you are standing in front of a Victoria-Georgian style house, you will get the impression that the house looks strict and compact. Such a house has usually two stories, but there are rarely open patios or verandas around the house.

The Jamaican-Georgian style has the lines of the Victorian-Georgian style with a tropical influence and verandas at the house sides. A good example for this style is the Devon House in Kingston.

When you have a boat and would like to dock it, you have two options: at the marina or at your own private dock. The option for a private dock is harder to find, because there are no artificial canals in Jamaica. The only option for you in this case is a beachfront property with a berth into the open sea.

When you make your decision to purchase a house, you have to find out if your new property is fully equipped with all appliances and if the furniture is included. If this is not the case, then your dream house will get more expensive, because you have furnish the interior and maybe renovate a little bit.

For the calculation of the transfer tax and the stamp duty, the furniture is not relevant because they are chattel and do not need to be separated from the purchase price like in other countries e.g. Cayman Islands.

The transfer tax in Jamaica is like the annual property tax calculated based on the unimproved land value, and stamp duty is based on the purchase price.

There are differences to consider when buying a single-family home or a home or a condominium in a strata community, and your agent should explain these differences to you during your purchase process. Strata is the term for a condominium development.

In case you are new to Jamaica, you should ask your real estate agent about the utility companies in your target location area. When your new home is in a strata community, some of these service providers are already contracted by the strata association, and you have to pay for them with your monthly maintenance fees.

You will need to register with the companies that provide services like water, sewer, electricity, cable, and trash removal. Telephone may not be necessary because the cell phone and Wi-Fi network is good. While we were driving around on the island, we always had a good connection, even in the mountains. However, when you have a hot spot with a service contract from your home country, it is a good idea to use a local SIM card for your internet service, because otherwise you may experience slow service from your provider and high roaming costs.

With this brief overview, you are ready to make your wish list for your dream home. You will need this list not only for your meeting with the real estate agent but also for your meeting with your mortgage officer at the bank.

Based on this wish list, the mortgage officer can give you an introduction to the mortgage process in Jamaica and tell you what kinds of documents you must present when you apply for your mortgage. You also should ask for a good faith estimate of what kinds of costs and expenses to expect at the closing table.

Title Types in Jamaica

When you purchase a property in Jamaica, you need to know a few details about the real estate titles.

Every piece of land in Jamaica is recorded on the tax roll at the National Land Agency, and the government guarantees these titles. That means the lot has a description with the owner's name, the address of the lot, and a valuation number as well as the survey report for the specific property.

The annual tax assessment for each registered property is based on the numeric code, and the annual tax bill is sent to the current owner of the property. The taxes for a piece of property are calculated on the basis of the unimproved land value with mass appraisal techniques.

However, only 55 percent of all pieces of land are correctly registered with the National Land Agency, and the rightful owner has as proof of his or her land ownership a certificate of title. The rest of the landowners are a little bit in limbo, because they have to prove their ownership in case they would like to sell their property or get a mortgage from a lender.

The government encourages the people to properly register their piece of land with the Land Administration and Management Program and get a certificate of title. This certificate will make it much easy for them to sell or to put a lien on the property or get a building permit for their new home.

Every landowner is entitled to this certificate of title and can register his piece of land. This process needs documentation such as proof of ownership like a purchase receipt and time for the examination of the documents. When the proper fees and charges are paid, the owner gets his or her copy of the Certificate of Title; the original stays with the agency.

In this centralized registry, all encumbrances, liens, and restrictions are recorded. Most importantly, it is noted when a purchase contract for a property is pending, and that is a good protection for the future property owner.

Commonly a property is titled to a natural person; however, for tax purposes in your home country, or for business purposes, you can also take the title in a corporation's name. In such cases, you should definitely seek the advice of an attorney and your accountant to evaluate the best option for your legal and tax situation.

The real estate property can be transferred as a fee simple or leasehold, and these kinds of titles refer to a single-family home.

When you buy a fee simple property, you own the lot, including the building that is located on that piece of land. But when you purchase a leasehold property, you own the house but not the piece of land on which the house is standing. The land belongs to someone else, and when the land lease is up, the building on the lot goes back together with the land to the lease holder. In such a purchase case, it is important to evaluate when the land lease is up.

The fee simple properties are usually not located in a strata association community, and they have no monthly maintenance fee.

The leasehold properties usually have a third party who is entitled to an annuity for the land lease.

The third kind of title is the strata title. This kind of title is used in condominium complexes. In this title, the land owner who is in the first place of all owners is liable for the total amount of the taxes. However, the other owners of the strata have to contribute their share, and the process of this payment is described in the bylaws of the strata.

You have to check for this process when buying a unit in a strata. There are also other costs that apply, and the residents of the strata as a whole have to pay for these expenses so that the strata complex is properly managed. These monthly expenses are the maintenance fees.

The members of the strata cooperation own the building complex as a whole, and each individual owner gets only a share of the whole development. How this individual unit ownership is regulated and titled and how you can mortgage such a unit is also stated in the condominium documents. The best information source for these details is either your agent or your attorney.

Getting a Mortgage in Jamaica

You have the dream to purchase a home on a tropical island, but you do not have enough liquidity to pay for this dream home in cash. In this case your only option for success is a mortgage.

Before you can apply for a mortgage, you need to open a bank account, and for this task, you need some documentation so that you can prove who you are.

You will need your passport or driver's license with a picture, and a second ID like a credit card. As proof of your residency, you will need utility bills and recent bank statements and at least two local references when you are a Jamaican citizen. As a foreign national, you must provide notarized references from reputable sources.

This is not the complete document list, because each bank has its own documentation requirements. For details you can contact us by email so that we can discuss your requirements.

Usually your bank account will get interest payments each month. To get these interests payments, you have to meet the minimum balance requirements. The monthly charges for the account are also waived when your account meets the average balance requirements.

As a foreign national, you have the option to open an account in your home country currency with the same above-mentioned terms. You can make unlimited and free-of-charge money transfers between your different accounts in the Jamaican bank.

With the opening of your bank account, you have fulfilled your first step to apply for a mortgage.

When the moment for the mortgage application arrives, then you also need a TRN number. That is the tax registration number from the tax administration, and it shows that you are a taxpayer in Jamaica. As soon as you earn income in Jamaica, even as a foreign national, you have to request this number.

Another very important detail in the mortgage application process is the verification of your monthly income. The verification papers can be tax returns or monthly income statements from your employer. There will be further documents along the application path, but these papers are mostly lender specific and can change quickly, so we do not list them here. All requested documents have to be in English.

You also should check with your lender if there are any age restrictions for the mortgage, because before a certain age and after a certain birthday, you will not get a loan. In such an age-related case, you will have to pay for your dream home in cash.

Under the above circumstances, it is best to start the mortgage application process before you even start looking for your new home. Such a preapproval process for a mortgage can take about two weeks.

Your real estate professional in Jamaica will also ask you for your mortgage preapproval letter before he or she works with you. Based on their code of ethics, the Realtors are obligated to screen the potential buyers for a property before they show any house to them.

When you start the mortgage approval process, you should shop around at different Jamaican banks that operate in the lending business with foreign nationals. The mortgage interest rates and terms vary in the different banks; however, the paperwork is similar.

The interest rates for mortgages in Jamaica are decided by the Bank of Jamaica, who has supervising functions in this matter. The usual mortgage terms are two, three, twenty, or thirty years. Besides these terms, there are many further details to consider when using a mortgage. One important point in this regard is the early repayment penalty.

Such a repayment penalty can be costly, and therefore you should check with your lender about what their regulation is in this part. Get this important information from your lender in writing; otherwise, you cannot prove this agreed term when the early repayment occurs, and you can have an unpleasant discussion at that time.

Usually the lender requires 10 percent down payment in a purchase transaction plus the expenses that arise during the transaction. The above-mentioned down payment relates to a local Jamaican resident, so as a foreign national, you should expect higher down payment requirements. Therefore be prepared to provide 40 to 50 percent of the purchase price as down payment, and the rest can be financed.

Many lenders also require life insurance for the term of the mortgage so that in case anything happens to you, the borrower, the mortgage is covered and can be repaid with the proceeds of that life insurance. The bank accepts any life insurance as long as it is assignable to the lender.

When you are looking for such a life insurance policy, you should keep in mind that a term life insurance is less expensive and will offer the mortgage protection that you need. An insurance professional will certainly help you with this matter.

On the mortgage amount, there is a stamp duty due when the money is paid at the transaction closing. The duty amount depends on the mortgage amount.

To protect yourself, you should definitely hire an attorney to represent you during the purchase process. The seller's attorney will write the contract in the best interest of the seller. Your attorney's task is to ensure that your own interests in this transaction are well observed and that you have no legal problems after the closing with your new dream home. This attorney's expenses are not part of the direct closing costs, and you have to pay them out of your pocket.

For the evaluation of the property value of your home, the lender will order a special report from an approved surveyor and appraiser. The task ensures that you get what you pay for and that you know the fair market value for your land inclusive of the building on it.

This specific report is not only a security for you, but also a necessity for your lender because it has to make sure that the property is worth what you are borrowing. The expenses for these reports are your buyer expenses.

When you have completed your application, the lender will preapprove you for a mortgage. Now you are prepared for your meeting with the real estate professional.

Realtor Association in Jamaica

The Realtors Association of Jamaica (RAJ) was formerly the Jamaica Association of Real Estate Brokers and Appraisers and was established in 1966. At that time there were no regulations or rules for this business sector, and the association created a regulatory framework to conduct their business.

Today the RAJ is the only professional organization throughout Jamaica. All members of this association hold a dealers and/or salesman license issued by the real estate board. This regulatory body was established in 1987 based on an act of parliament.

The Realtors Association of Jamaica is affiliated with the National Association of Realtors (NAR) in the United States, and the Jamaican Realtors can join the NAR as an international member. However, this opportunity does not exist for the foreign Realtors who would like to join the Jamaican Realtors as an international member.

The association updates and adapts its procedures and conduct of business practice constantly. The association has its own code of ethics, which is adapted from the NAR code of ethics. Each member is bound to this code and works on that basis.

The real estate code of ethics is probably not the same in your home country. That means you cannot assume that client right such as confidentiality or protection of your information are the same as in your country. The legal requirements and business rules are totally different. You will get more details on this topic in the chapter Home Hunt in Jamaica.

The members of the Jamaica Realtors have access to a Multiple Listing Service (MLS), and every member can use it. Since 2010 the listings in the Jamaica MLS are automatically transferred to the international website of Realtor.com in the United States. However, the Jamaican Realtors are not obligated to do so, and therefore the publicly marketed properties are only a limited selection of available properties.

The entry into the MLS in Jamaica does secure a commission for a cooperating broker in Jamaica; however, there may be changes in the commission split. The compensation for a listing is usually 5 percent plus 16½ percent general consumption tax.

The compensation between the cooperating Jamaican real estate professionals needs to be in writing, only to make sure that the commission will be paid and when. An international real estate broker may be entitled to a referral fee, but this fee needs to be negotiated with the Jamaican real estate professional.

In November 2015, there were 729 real estate members in the Realtors Association. In Jamaica the office managing brokers are called Realtors, and their sales agents are called Realtor Associates or dealers. Every member needs to be licensed and to be a member of the RAJ. The name Realtor is based on the NAR trademark and its rights.

In November 2015, there were 2,538 listings for sale and 382 properties for rent available on the international website of realtor.com. These listings were automatically transferred from the Jamaica MLS. Not included in this number are the properties that are not entered in the MLS. These listings are considered pocket listings, and they are not openly marketed.

As already mentioned, it is necessary to visit several agents' websites because every Realtor or Realtor associate only shows their own MLS listings on their websites. There is no public access for the entire MLS database in Jamaica. Real estate professionals who are not a member of the Realtor Association of Jamaica are unable to look into the MLS at all, because the MLS view is limited to the paying association members.

To become a Realtor or dealer, the real estate professional has to pass the education exam and to provide several reputation references before he or she can apply for a license at the real estate board. Continuing education is required every two years, and the payment of the license fee is mandatory to keep the existing license active.

Home Hunt in Jamaica

Now you know how to get ready for your house hunt in Jamaica, and you have your preapproval letter from your mortgage lender in your pocket. You are ready to go with your real estate agent on the home search and showings.

However, here are some details to know when selecting a real estate professional. As already mentioned in the chapter above, you will only see the listings of the Realtor office on each agent's website. Only your potential real estate agent has the view on the entire MLS database with all listed properties.

This said, you need to keep in mind that you are speaking with the listing agent of the property you are looking at. This agent has a confidentiality relationship with the seller, and as long as he or she does not have a confidentiality agreement signed with you, you should be careful what you are telling to the agent. Your private information may go to the seller of the listing, because the agent is the seller's representative.

Before you disclose any personal details to the real estate agent, you have to find out his or her relationship to the seller, and if there may be a dual representation toward you and the seller. A dual representation is not explicitly excluded in the real estate business rules in Jamaica.

Another important detail is to find out who is paying for your agent—the seller or yourself. Usually there is a commission commitment, when a property is listed on the MLS in Jamaica; however, this commitment can be altered during the process. Make sure that you have an agreement with your agent. That agreement should clearly state what your agent is doing for you and what you have to pay for it, when there is not an equal commission split in the transaction.

Based on your wish list, the real estate agent will research the Jamaica MLS database for the best matching properties on the market. At this moment you will already know if you want to buy an existing home or if you would like to build your own dream home.

Let us assume you want to buy an existing property. That can be a house or condominium, and you have to decide if you want to buy a newly constructed one or a resale.

When you buy a newly constructed home, you often can move in right away without spending too much money for renovation. Everything is new and in good shape, and it is hopefully energy efficient.

With an older home, you often have some issues to resolve before you move in. You at least have to do some painting. However, often you have more to do than that—maybe updating the kitchen and bathrooms and/or installing new appliances.

On your wish list, you certainly have written what your priorities are and how much you want to spend for your home.

Here are some priorities that you should keep in close focus. You have to tell your real estate agent these details at the beginning of your house hunt:

1.   Is the home that you want your primary residence or a vacation home?

2.   Do you want to have a house or a condominium/strata unit?

3.   How many bedrooms and bathrooms do you want?

4.   Do you want a garage?

5.   Do you want a yard?

6.   Do you want to have a boat?

7.   Do you want to renovate?

8.   Do you have children who need to go to school?

9.   How much do you want to spend for your new home?

This is a short but important wish list for your home in Jamaica. Now let us see why these questions are relevant.

When the home is your primary residence, then you intend to live in Jamaica year-round. In this case you must have the immigration status for a permanent residency on the island. Some important information on this topic is explained in the chapter Living and Working in Jamaica.

If your home is a vacation domicile, your immigration status is not relevant because you can easily come to the island for at least thirty days. In this case you need to have a ticket back to your home country and sufficient funds to support yourself during your stay in Jamaica.

When you are living all year in Jamaica, a house may be the best option. In a home you can do whatever you want, and you only have to pay for your utilities, annual taxes, and homeowner insurance. For the yard maintenance, you can hire a service company, if you do not want to do it yourself.

The maintenance task may tip the scale more to a condominium/strata home. Such a strata community can consist of homes or condominiums, and the maintenance tasks are often included in the monthly maintenance fees to the strata association so that you do not have to worry about the maintenance.

In a strata community with single houses or condominiums, you have to check what is included in the monthly maintenance fees and how the annual tax liability is regulated for your property. The details on the topic of taxes is already mentioned in the chapter Title Types in Jamaica.

Information on this topic is provided in the strata documents that the seller or the strata association provide to you. It is important to examine these documents carefully, because you will get details about your home insurance policy and what this insurance may cover. Sometimes the insurance of the association covers appliances like refrigerators or ranges in the units. When not, then you are on your own and have to insure these items yourself.

When you buy a condominium in a strata community, you get a portion of the whole complex. That means the complex and all units belong to all condominium owners. All owners together are responsible for the maintenance of the strata complex. To get this task done, every owner has to pay a monthly maintenance fee that covers the costs for the exterior and interior common areas. Your condominium unit in this strata complex is a portion of the whole, so you are automatically obligated to pay these monthly fees.

The condominium unit that you purchase in one of these strata communities should be separately titled; otherwise, you may not be able get a mortgage for the purchase because the lender has no possibility to secure its loan with the property.

One question above is the number of bedrooms and bathrooms. This is certainly easy to answer when you know how many people are in your family. Each person should have a bedroom and at least one bathroom for two people.

When you have to decide if you need a garage, please keep in mind that it is very hot in Jamaica during the day, and a garage can keep your car cool. A garage is also good protection for your own car in case you only stay part-time in Jamaica.

We have already discussed yard maintenance, and we should come back to this point. When you are only on vacation in Jamaica, you may consider a service company that will take care of your yard while you are absent. Such a service will cost money and will increase your annual holding expenses for your home.

The answers to the questions about a boat and schoolage children can limit your location options in Jamaica. When you are a foreign national, your children may not have all education options throughout the island and in this case the school options should have a high priority in your house hunt.

Jamaica has no artificial canals for boats. When you intend to have your boat close by, you need to buy a property close to the coastline and build your own private dock. Such a construction project is at some places easier and less costly than at others. You have to examine the shoreline before you buy. The easiest solution for your boat is a place in one of the marinas in Jamaica, even when you have to drive there from your home.

For the question of how much you want to spend, you should know if you can and if you want to renovate your home. If you are a handyman and you can do some repairs and updates yourself, then you can look for a home that is cheaper because of its exterior and interior conditions.

If you are not that good with your own hands, a perfectly renovated home might be the better choice for you, but this option comes with a higher price tag.

Let us now talk about the price that you can afford, and you can make a quick calculation for yourself.

Let us assume you want to buy a property for US$200,000, and you intend to put 40 percent down. You have to bring additional money for the closing expenses to the table. The transaction costs are usually not included in the financing of a property and must be paid out of pocket.

When you have discussed all the above questions with your real estate professional, he or she will be able to find matching homes in Jamaica. When you have found a nice property selection, you will have showings together with your agent.

After you have done some showings, you will certainly find the perfect dream home. Your agent will contact the seller, and his or her attorney will write the sale contract for your dream home. This contract will be sent to you, and you have to review the contract. Unless you are a real estate attorney in Jamaica yourself, you should definitely hire your own attorney to ensure, that your interest in this transaction is protected.

When all terms and conditions in the contract for this transaction are reviewed by you and your attorney and meet your expectations, then you sign the contract and return it to the seller. The seller signs the document too, and your attorney will get a copy of the signed contract for your files.

When you have signed the contract, commonly 15 percent of the purchase price plus parts of the closing costs are paid into a trust account.

With the legally binding contract, which is also called the agreement for sale, you have to start your work toward the closing table. The normal period for such a closing preparation is ninety to one hundred twenty days, because of the paperwork that is necessary for the transfer of the property.

At the closing the so-called instrument of transfer is signed by buyer and seller, and the involved attorneys sign as witnesses. Then the balance of the purchase price is paid, and the seller hands over the keys.

For the preparation of the lender's closing documents, the signed agreement for sale is provided to the lender. The lending institution starts their mortgage process with this agreement.

Details to this part of the transaction are explained in the chapters Mortgage Process in Jamaica and Purchase Statement for the Transaction.

Home Inspection and Site Survey— Two Important Tasks

When you have made the decision which property you want to buy and have the agreement for sale with the seller, it is time to start your own activities in the transaction. The lender is already working on the legal and mortgage-related tasks. In this chapter we focus on your tasks that are not in the scope of the lender.

Like in many countries, you should order a professional home inspection and a survey for your future home site. The survey is very important when you buy a property to make sure that the land that you want to buy is exactly what you contracted for. Only 55 percent of the properties in Jamaica are properly registered to the current owner, and you certainly want to get a good and clean title—right?

When you purchase a condominium, there is only one parcel number for the entire condominium complex. All owners together are liable for the total property tax amount, and you as the condominium unit owner have to pay your particular share of this amount. There must be a process in place in the condominium complex for this part, and you should check with the strata association to see how this process works in your complex.

The complex itself should be surveyed during the construction process and should be properly registered with the government; therefore, you can check with the land registry and verify if a survey is necessary. You can also ask the strata association for a copy of the survey report.

The second task for you is the home inspection, and this task is strongly recommended. You assure yourself about what condition your new home is in. It is important to know if the house is well maintained and how much renovation or remodeling you have to expect in the near future.

In case you find damages at the home, you can negotiate with the former owner and make him or her pay for necessary repairs or ask for a price reduction, whatever you like best.

During the home inspection, the inspector examines the home construction as well as the exterior and interior features of the house, including the roof and the foundation.

The tropical climate requires a proper pest-control protection for the property; therefore, you should evaluate the condition of your new property in this regard.

When your new home is located in a homeowner community, you should request evidence that the association fees are paid and that there are no open assessments or unpaid charges from the former owner.

Another good idea is to request a copy of the monthly water and electricity bills to find out how much the monthly utility payments are and to ensure that all utility bills are paid in full until the closing.

For your protection as the buyer of a home, pay attention to these tasks and discuss the results with your attorney.

For the site survey and the home inspection, you have to pay out of your own pocket. These expenses are not directly connected to the mortgage process, and they are not part of the transaction settlement bill.

Mortgage Process in Jamaica

With the legally binding contract, you have to start your work with the lender to finalize your mortgage process until the closing date. The normal period for such a closing preparation is ninety to one hundred and twenty days.

As already mentioned, you will need to provide several personal and financial documents for the mortgage process. The first part of documentation you have done before you started your house hunt. The result of this process was the preapproval, which tells you how much you can borrow based on your financial situation. With the preapproval letter in your hand, you are a well-regarded potential buyer to the property seller.

Now you already have chosen your property and signed the contract, your lender will start its work for the mortgage payout and the collateralization of the mortgage with your new property. These activities include all tasks for the title search and checks of the title documents, as well as the registration with the government and transfer preparation including the document for the transfer. The lender's attorney is in charge of these tasks and will also pay the necessary fees and charges for the title transfer. Details about the fees and charges are listed in the next chapter.

Your tasks in this step are to provide all documents for the lender, so that the payout of the mortgage can be finished in a timely manner at the date of property transfer.

Here are some details that you have to work on:

- Obtain life insurance that will cover the mortgage, in case something happens to you.

- Make a decision about what kind of mortgage you want to have for your property purchase, which interest rate, and the length of the repayment of the mortgage.

- You have to deposit your portion of the purchase price into an account with your lender. As a foreign national, this amount can be up to 50 percent of the purchase price.

It will help when you can get a photocopy of the certificate of title from the seller and the original of the surveyor's identification report. In case these documents are not available, the lender will certainly take care of these papers; however, you will have to pay for them.

For the mortgage that you get from your lender, you have to pay stamp duty for the registration in the governmental registry. This expense, like all the others, will be paid as soon as the mortgage papers are signed, and you do not have to worry about it.

Besides these fees that are connected to the real estate transaction, there are some smaller-cost items involved, like life insurance assignment or miscellaneous legal expenses, and the lender usually charges a lending commitment fee.

Purchase Statement for the Transaction

To give you a better idea of how much money you will need in addition to the purchase price, we created the following example of a closing statement for a mortgage.

In this example, we buy a home for US$200,000 and finance the deal with US$120,000. We choose in the example US dollars as the currency and not Jamaican dollars, because the numbers are easier to read, and the calculation is easier to follow.

The statement shows your buyer numbers at closing day. Some of these costs are only 50 percent of the whole amount, because based on the legal regulations, the buyer and seller share the costs. The shared costs are marked in the following statement.

The transfer tax of 5 percent of the property's market value is not included in this statement, because this tax is paid entirely by the seller. The real estate commission is usually paid the same way.

Description	Calculation	Amount US$
Down Payment	40%	80,000.00
Loan Amount	60%	120,000.00
Stamp Duty on Purchase price (split 50/50 between seller/buyer)	4%	4,000.00
Recording Fee for Title (split 50/50 between seller and buyer)	0.5%	500.00
Attorney's Fees + 16.5% Gen. Consumption. Tax	3%	6,990.00
Annual Tax Prorated (Tax is paid quarterly)	est.	500.00
Mortgage Duty on Loan Amount	est.	750.00
Miscellaneous, legal expenses	est.	1,500.00
Total		214,240.00

As you see, the total amount of the real estate transaction is US$214,240. From this amount, there is only US$120,000 covered by the loan, the rest—the US$80,000 down payment and US$14,240 of additional costs—has to come out of your pocket. These additional costs are around 7½ percent of the purchase price.

The total of this transaction is due on the closing date, and the closing date is set as soon as all necessary documents are ready for the signature. The instrument of transfer is signed by the buyer and seller and witnessed by the parties' attorneys.

When you buy your property with cash, the previous closing statement will vary, because not all costs may apply. In such a cash transaction, you have to negotiate which attorney is in charge of the legal transfer tasks, so that you become the owner of a free and clean title.

Building Your Dream Home in Jamaica

Maybe you will not find your dream home among the listed homes; maybe the existing homes are too small or too old or not at the right place. Whatever the reason may be, you still have an excellent chance to get what you want: build your own dream home.

When you get ready for your building project, you have to ask yourself the same questions as when you buy a home. Sit down and draw your dream home as an outline. In this outline, you put in your bedrooms, kitchen, bathrooms, living area, and so on. You decide if you want one story or more, a garage, maybe a private dock, and your desired location, and most importantly, you consider your budget.

In case you want to make your dream house as energy efficient as possible, the insulation of the exterior construction and the location of the windows are very important. You can enhance your energy savings with covered porches and shade trees in the yard. Another option is the use of a sustainable energy source like solar panels.

When you plan your landscaping, you should prefer native plants and trees, because they need less watering. You should invest a little time to investigate the best options for your specific region.

Your benefit when you build your own dream home is that you will get exactly what you want, and this can be even cheaper than when you purchase a finished home. You also know what kind of material was used during the construction process, and you will have no repairs or maintenance for the first few years.

Now you know how your dream home looks in your mind, and you have to start making it real. To evaluate your preferred location, you should go there and observe it carefully, to ensure everything in the neighborhood makes you happy.

During your observation trips, you can look for a piece of land that you can purchase. This is the time to contact a real estate agent and search for the perfect piece of land to build your dream home. Maybe this piece of land is listed on the MLS.

The agent can also provide you with important land information, like the size and zoning details, so that you can check firsthand if your desired dream home will fit into these governmental guidelines.

In the event that you and your agent find the perfect spot for your new home, you make an offer for the purchase of the land. The process for the transaction is similar to the purchase of an existing house, as already explained, with a few differences.

Now you have your piece of land, and the purchase process has taken its first legal steps. While you are waiting for your closing of the land purchase, you can start planning for your dream home.

With your raw outline, you go to an architect who will assist you with the construction plans. The architect will draw your home as you want it to be. When you want to have an energy-efficient home that saves you money over the long run, it is a good idea to put details like solar panels into your construction plans.

During this planning and drawing phase, your architect will listen to your wishes and match them with the building codes and regulations of your target region. The existing building act in Jamaica is vague, and every parish (these are the administrative districts or regions) has the right to make its own regulations in the form of bylaws.

As soon as your plans are ready, you should check with the local building department about which permits and inspections are necessary for your building project. The regulations for permitting and licensing of professionals are in a reform process and in the implementation process everywhere. For your own protection, you should always investigate the rules, especially because Jamaica has earthquake safety and hurricane-protecting construction methods in place.

Always check with building departments and government agencies when starting a building project and hiring professionals for a construction project. Find out as much as you can about your potential contractors so that you are not sorry later, when something goes wrong.

These rules are even more important when you use a mortgage for your construction project. Lenders in Jamaica usually finance only 85 percent of a building project, when you are local, and they may have some additional requirements in such a financing process.

When your building project is successfully completed and passes all inspections, you will be a proud property owner in one of the nicest places in the Caribbean islands.

Rent Out Your Property in Jamaica

You now know how to purchase your dream home or build your own in Jamaica, and you are prepared for your successful real estate investment business.

What should you do with your property in the tropical island when you are not in Jamaica or when you have more than one property unit?

Those questions are easy to answer. You can rent your unit, which is easy to do. You can give your unit to a dealer or a dealer associate (that is the Jamaican name for Realtor) who will market your unit. Rental listings are exclusive listings, which are also put into the MLS. The agent who brings you the tenant also prescreens him or her and gets a commission for this service. The common payment for a rental service is one month's rent plus the general consumption tax of $16\frac{1}{2}$ percent. This is either paid by the landlord or the new tenant or both in the event of the signed lease. When there are two agents working together, the commission is usually split between them.

When you rent your property or properties in a professional way, you generate income in Jamaica, and you have to register with the tax authority. In this case you apply for a tax registration number, and this registration number is directly connected to you as the landlord. You are liable for all the taxes due in regard to your property leases.

In case you are intending to go into the rental business, you have to decide what types of tenants you are looking for. When you want to rent only to tourists and visitors on the island, you have to add the guest accommodation room tax and the general consumption tax to your rental bill. These taxes have to be paid to the government within thirty days.

This general consumption tax is 16½ percent and needs to be added to all services that are pursued for gain or income, and such a rental payment is by definition income. The accommodation room tax is US$1 per night and room and is to be paid when you host guests. For this tax, you do not need to be licensed under the Tourist Board Act. This tax matter applies only for tourists and visitors who stay for a few days.

When you lease your property to tenants who reside in your property for a month or longer, then you have to take the following steps:

You have to charge the general consumption tax for every rental monthly payment, and you have to pay stamp duty for your lease agreement when it is signed. When the lease agreement is only one month, there is only a flat rate; otherwise, the stamp duty is 1 percent of the annual lease payments.

Depending on your lease contracts, you have to specify to tenants what costs are included in the rent and what expenses need to be paid by the tenant.

These expenses are electricity, water, telephone, TV, cable, and maintenance. You should carefully separate the utility costs and the rental payment, because of the tax and stamp duty implications.

The landlord is responsible for the homeowner's insurance that covers the interior of the unit and exterior of the building and the maintenance of the property, like landscaping. In addition, the tenant has to insure his or her personal belongings inside the rental unit separately.

When you rent your unit fully furnished, you should have an inventory list that clearly states what belongs to the unit so that you have proof in case something is missing after the tenant leaves.

Also, be very clear if you as the landlord accept pets and smokers. When your rental property is located in an apartment complex, you have to check with your association and the association documents of your unit. In these documents, you will find the necessary details about the rental process and the limitations.

Depending on the location, size, and type of rental property, your rental income can vary greatly throughout the island. When you purchase your property, you should conduct a little research in the direct neighborhood or with your rental agent. However, based on our own research in 2015, you can calculate as a rule of thumb US$2 per square foot monthly.

With the beginning of the lease period, the landlord is entitled to the first month's rent and a security deposit. You have to communication which types of payments you accept, especially when you do not manage the unit yourself but with the help of an agent or a management company. Usually the tenant can pay in cash, with a credit card, or electronically. You have to find out which payment method is the best for you and your tenant.

As already mentioned, there are homeowner's insurance, general consumption tax, stamp duty, and accommodation room tax involved in the rental process. Besides these expenses, you have to pay annual property tax for your property. The property tax is assessed on the unimproved land value.

For the income that you earn with rental units in Jamaica, there is income tax due. The personal income tax is 25 percent. This percentage is applied on the total income less the allowed deductions. The costs that are allowed to subtract from your Jamaican income are different than in your home country; therefore, you will need a local accountant who can assist you with this matter.

Besides the income tax in Jamaica, your generated income may be taxable in your home country, and the paid taxes in Jamaica can possibly be deducted for your tax amount due in your home country. There are often tax agreements between different countries, and each country has its own procedure in this matter.

You have to pay attention to the different tax regulations about depreciation of the property and capital gain when selling the property in the future. Tax codes change often, and a local accountant, who is familiar with local and international tax regulations, will be your best friend in such a situation.

Is this something that interests you? Excellent! We can help you get this process started and make it successful. An email to our address at the end of the book is the best way to get in touch with us.

Your Benefits in Jamaica

We hope that we made you curious about Jamaica and that you come to explore this tropical island yourself. In this book we show you what to expect and how to enjoy your life here. You now know how to get started and be successful with your business venture.

Jamaica is one of the most sought-after destinations in the Caribbean islands because of its cultural diversity and lifestyle, real estate, and business opportunities, and it will offer you the same perks. With the right consulting partners, your wildest dreams can come true. You only have to decide to start.

Jamaica is an economically improving nation and welcomes every investment that brings employment and wealth to the country. For your direct investment in the projects and programs in Jamaica, you can receive government incentives and cooperation along your way. This cooperation will be beneficial for both parties—you and Jamaica.

Whatever your dreams are for your life, there is a way to realize these dreams.

Are you ready to start your adventure in Jamaica?

If the answer is yes, we are happy to assist you! You can reach us at the following websites and email addresses.

- Author website: www.andreahoffdomin.com
- Florida Dream Homes: www.florida-dream-homes.net; email: andrea@florida-informations.com

If Jamaica is not the right country for your business and private ventures, check out our other books about Caribbean topics and regions e.g. Florida and Cayman Island. To get a better impression about Jamaica and its beauty, look into our picture book.

We thank you very much for your interest and your attention in this book. You are always welcome to contact us with questions and notes.

Best wishes from the Caribbean islands and the Sunshine State of Florida!

www.ingramcontent.com/pod-product-compliance
Lightning Source LLC
Chambersburg PA
CBHW050509210326
41521CB00011B/2393